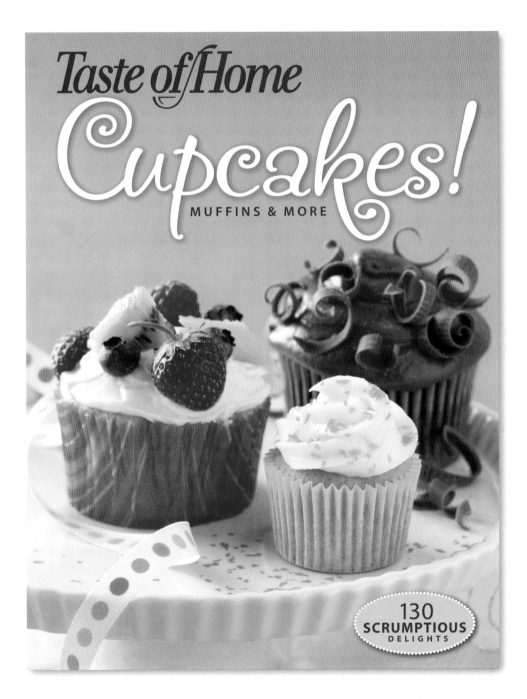

Taste of Home
Cupcakes!
MUFFINS & MORE

130
SCRUMPTIOUS
DELIGHTS

Editor:	Amy Glander
Art Director:	Rudy Krochalk
Layout Designers:	Kathy Crawford, Nancy Novak, Emma Acevedo
Content Production Supervisor:	Julie Wagner
Proofreader:	Linne Bruskewitz
Editorial Assistant:	Barb Czysz
Recipe Asset Management System:	Coleen Martin (Manager), Sue A. Jurack (Specialist)
Indexer:	Julie Schnittka
Food Director:	Diane Werner
Test Kitchen Manager:	Karen Scales
Recipe Editors:	Mary King, Christine Rukavena
Studio Photographers:	Rob Hagen (Senior), Dan Roberts, Jim Wieland, Lori Foy
Food Stylists:	Sarah Thompson (Senior), Kaitlyn Basasie, Alynna Malson (Assistant)
Set Stylists:	Jennifer Bradley Vent (Senior), Stephanie Marchese (Senior), Melissa Haberman, Dee Dee Jacq
Photo Studio Coordinator:	Kathleen Swaney
Senior Editor/Books:	Mark Hagen
Creative Director:	Ardyth Cope
Vice President, Executive Editor/Books:	Heidi Reuter Lloyd
Editor in Chief:	Catherine Cassidy
President, Food & Entertaining:	Suzanne M. Grimes
President and Chief Executive Officer:	Mary G. Berner
Cover Photography:	Rob Hagen (Photographer), Melissa Haberman (Set Stylist), Diane Armstrong (Food Stylist)
Stock Photography:	Cupcake Illustration (p. 5), M. Jackson/Shutterstock.com Bottom Right Cupcake Photo (p. 6), Darren K. Fisher/Shutterstock.com Top Left Cupcake Photo (p. 7), Darren K. Fisher/Shutterstock.com

©2008 Reiman Media Group, LLC
5400 S. 60th Street
Greendale, WI 53129

International Standard Book Number (10): 0-89821-624-9
International Standard Book Number (13): 978-0-89821-624-0
Library of Congress Control Number: 2008928966

Pictured on front cover: Berry-Topped White Cupcakes (p. 32), Chocolate Cupcakes (p. 12), Amaretto Dream Cupcakes (p. 10)

Pictured on back cover: Lemon Curd Cupcakes (p. 86), Berry Mini Breads (p. 104)

Great Gift!

Cupcakes! Muffins & More makes a great gift for those who are crazy for cupcakes or simply love baking. To order additional copies, specify item number 38530 and send $14.99 (plus $4.99 shipping/processing for one book, $5.99 for two or more) to: Shop Taste of Home, Suite 197, P.O. Box 26820, Lehigh Valley, PA 18002-6820. To order by credit card, call toll-free 1-800/880-3012.

Indulge your fancy with **130 dreamy** miniature sensations!

Posy Cupcakes (p. 27)

Tender, fluffy, and oh-so-sweet, there's nothing like a petite cake confection crowned with icing to make hearts smile. Whether you're a cupcake connoisseur, go mad for fresh-from-the-oven muffins or simply enjoy a delicious slice of your favorite mini bread, it's easy to create a little piece of heaven with the irresistible, pop-in-your-mouth baked treats in *Cupcakes!*.

Cupcakes! features everything from easy-to-make classic delights that bake up in a jiffy to whimsical creations kids will go crazy for. Discover freshly frosted Amaretto Dream Cupcakes (p. 10), have a blast creating playful Posy Cupcakes (p. 27), splurge on warm Cream Cheese Apple Muffins (p. 56) and keep taste buds tickled with a loaf of Banana Split Bread (p. 100).

And to top it off, you'll find a mammoth assortment of big-batch delights and prize-winning favorites…so there's no need to be frazzled the next time you have to whip up a yummy treat for a potluck, bake sale or classroom party.

With flavorful recipes, inspirational ideas and easy baking and decorating tips, you simply can't go wrong with this collection of delectable goodies. We know you'll turn to this treasury of blissful bites whenever you're seeking to satisfy your sweet tooth. So grab this book and run to the kitchen…*happiness awaits!*

Table of Contents

Mint Brownie Cupcakes (p. 69)

Fabulous Frostings

All it takes is one lip-smacking bite into a frosted cupcake to bring a surge of delight to anyone with a serious sweet tooth. There are, however, a few simple tricks of the trade that make frosting cupcakes easy and fun.

The first thing to know when making a homemade frosting is to always thoroughly sift the confectioners' sugar prior to blending it with other frosting ingredients. If there are any lumps in the sugar, there will be lumps in the frosting, which will clog decorating tips. Frosting needs to be just the right consistency for spreading and decorating. If it's too thin, add a little confectioners' sugar. If it's too thick, add a little milk.

The second secret is that you can decorate like a pro with cake decorating tips and pastry or resealable plastic bags. Begin by filling a pastry or resealable plastic bag with room-temperature frosting. Place the bag in a measuring cup and roll down the top edge to make a cuff. Smooth the filling down toward the tip to remove any air bubbles, which will cause breaks in the design when piping. Twist the top of the bag shut.

Cut a small hole in the corner of the bag and insert a decorating tip. Reinforce the seal between the bag and tip with tape or a plastic coupler. The coupler allows you to easily change decorating tips for a variety of designs. Have fun experimenting using different tips. You can create pinwheels, stars, flowers, swirls, leaves, vines, polka dots, letters and shell or scalloped borders, just to name a few. For more simple decorations, just snip the corner off the filled resealable plastic bag and pipe away.

Don't forget to release your inner artist by having fun with color! Tint white frosting to any color of the rainbow using liquid, gel or paste food coloring. Liquid will give a pastel color; gel and paste give a deeper color. Add a little at a time, stir in and check the color. You can always add more to darken a color, but be advised it's difficult to lighten. The color generally darkens as the frosting dries.

VANILLA FROSTING

Mary Faulk, Cambridge, Wisconsin

2	cups confectioners' sugar
2	tablespoons butter, softened
2	tablespoons milk
1/2	teaspoon vanilla extract

◆ In a bowl, combine the sugar, butter, milk and vanilla. Beat on medium speed until smooth and fluffy. Spread over cupcakes.

YIELD: 1 CUP.

FREEZER FROSTING

Evelyn Comeau, Virden, Manitoba

1/3	cup shortening
4-1/2	cups confectioners' sugar, *divided*
1-1/2	teaspoons vanilla extract
1/4	teaspoon salt
3/4	to 1 cup heavy whipping cream

◆ In a bowl, cream shortening, 1 cup of sugar, vanilla and salt. Add the remaining sugar alternately with whipping cream. Beat until the frosting reaches desired consistency. Cover and freeze for up to 2 months. Thaw before frosting cupcakes.

YIELD: ABOUT 3 CUPS.

BAKERY FROSTING

Barbara Jones, Pana, Illinois

2	cups shortening
1/2	cup powdered nondairy creamer
1	teaspoon almond extract
1	package (32 ounces) confectioners' sugar
1/2	to 3/4 cup water

Food coloring, optional

◆ In a large bowl, beat the shortening, creamer and extract. Gradually beat in confectioners' sugar. Add enough water until frosting reaches desired consistency. If desired, add food coloring. Store in the refrigerator for up to 3 months. Bring to room temperature before spreading.

YIELD: 8 CUPS.

CHOCOLATE MOUSSE FROSTING

Kim Marie Van Rheenen, Mendota, Illinois

- 1 cup cold fat-free milk
- 1 package (1.4 ounces) sugar-free instant chocolate fudge pudding mix
- 1 carton (8 ounces) frozen reduced-fat whipped topping, thawed

◆ In a bowl, beat milk and pudding mix on low speed for 2 minutes. Fold in whipped topping. Frost cupcakes.

YIELD: 3-1/2 CUPS.

BRIDAL CAKE FROSTING

Joanne Leistico, Elk River, Minnesota

- 10 cups shortening, *divided*
- 35 cups confectioners' sugar (about 10 pounds), *divided*
- 2-1/2 cups milk, *divided*
- 10 teaspoons vanilla extract, *divided*
- 5 teaspoons almond extract, *divided*

◆ In a large bowl, cream 2 cups shortening. Gradually beat in 7 cups confectioners' sugar. Add 1/2 cup milk; beat until light and fluffy. Beat in 2 teaspoons vanilla and 1 teaspoon almond extract. Repeat four times. Store in the refrigerator. Bring to room temperature before decorating cupcakes.

YIELD: 40 CUPS.

AMARETTO BUTTER FROSTING

Anette Stevens, Olds, Alberta

- 3 cups confectioners' sugar
- 1/4 cup butter, melted
- 3 to 4 tablespoons heavy whipping cream
- 2 to 3 tablespoons Amaretto

Yellow edible glitter, optional

◆ In a bowl, beat confectioners' sugar and butter. Add 3 tablespoons cream and 2 tablespoons Amaretto; beat until smooth. Add remaining cream and Amaretto if needed to achieve spreading consistency. Frost cupcakes. Sprinkle with edible glitter if desired.

YIELD: ABOUT 2-1/4 CUPS.

Classic Cupcakes

SPREAD A LITTLE love with these petite, fluffy treats guaranteed to warm hearts and bring big smiles. From frosted delights to cream-filled wonders, these blissful bites are simply confection perfection.

CHOCOLATE CUPCAKES, P. 12

AMARETTO DREAM CUPCAKES

These heavenly cupcakes feature the tempting flavors of almond and spice from Amaretto. They're the perfect treat to serve for dessert when entertaining friends. Add colored edible glitter for a finishing touch.

—Anette Stevens, Olds, Alberta

3/4   cup butter, softened
1-1/2 cups packed brown sugar
2   eggs
1/2 cup buttermilk
1/4 cup Amaretto
2 cups all-purpose flour
1-1/2 teaspoons baking powder
1/2 teaspoon baking soda
1/4 teaspoon salt
1/3 cup slivered almonds
Amaretto Butter Frosting
(see recipe on page 7)

◆ In a large bowl, cream the butter and brown sugar until light and fluffy. Add the eggs, one at a time, beating well after each addition.

◆ In a small bowl, combine buttermilk and Amaretto. Combine the flour, baking powder, baking soda and salt. Add to the creamed mixture alternately with buttermilk mixture, beating well after each addition. Stir in almonds.

◆ Fill paper-lined muffins cups two-thirds full. Bake at 375° for 14-16 minutes or until a toothpick comes out clean. Cool for 5 minutes before removing cupcakes from pans to cool completely. Frost with the Amaretto Butter Frosting.

YIELD: 24 SERVINGS.

PEANUT BUTTER CUP CUPCAKES

Kids love these rich, yummy cupcakes in school lunches or at parties. They're so easy to make because the mini peanut butter cups add just the right amount of sweetness so I don't have to spend extra time frosting them.

—Heidi Harrington, Steuben, Maine

1/3 cup shortening
1/3 cup peanut butter
1-1/4 cups packed brown sugar
2 eggs
1 teaspoon vanilla extract
1-3/4 cups all-purpose flour
1-3/4 teaspoons baking powder
1 teaspoon salt
1 cup milk
16 miniature peanut butter cups

◆ In a bowl, cream the shortening, peanut butter and brown sugar. Beat in eggs and vanilla. Combine the flour, baking powder and salt; add to creamed mixture alternately with milk.

◆ Fill paper-lined muffin cups with 1/4 cup of batter. Press a peanut butter cup into the center of each until top edge is even with batter. Bake at 350° for 22-24 minutes or until a toothpick inserted on an angle toward the center of the cupcakes comes out clean. Cool for 10 minutes before removing from pans to wire racks to cool completely.

YIELD: 16 SERVINGS.

CREAMY CENTER CUPCAKES

This recipe came from my mother, who made cupcakes from scratch when I was growing up. Sometimes she'd replace the smooth filling with homemade whipped cream, which was readily available on our farm.

—Caroline Anderson, Waupaca, Wisconsin

1 **package (18-1/4 ounces) devil's food cake mix**

3/4 **cup shortening**

2/3 **cup confectioners' sugar**

1 **cup marshmallow creme**

1 **teaspoon vanilla extract**

2 **cans (16 ounces *each*) chocolate frosting**

◆ Prepare and bake cake according to package directions for cupcakes, using paper-lined muffin cups. Cool for 10 minutes before removing from pans to wire racks to cool completely.

◆ Meanwhile, in a large bowl, cream shortening and sugar until light and fluffy. Add marshmallow creme and vanilla and mix well.

◆ Cut a small hole in the corner of a pastry or plastic bag; insert a very small tip. Fill the bag with cream filling. Push the tip through the bottom of paper-lined muffin cups to fill each cupcake. Frost cupcakes with chocolate frosting.

YIELD: 24 SERVINGS.

CHOCOLATE CUPCAKES

If you like chocolate, you're going to fall in love with these blissful cupcakes. Chocolate curls are a showy way to garnish these gorgeous gems.

—*Marlene Martin, Country Harbour Mines, Nova Scotia*

1/2	cup butter, softened
1	cup sugar
1	egg
1	teaspoon vanilla extract
1-1/2	cups all-purpose flour
1/2	cup baking cocoa
1	teaspoon baking soda
1/4	teaspoon salt
1/2	cup water
1/2	cup buttermilk

Frosting of your choice

◆ In a small bowl, cream butter and sugar until light and fluffy. Beat in egg and vanilla. Combine the flour, cocoa, baking soda and salt; add to creamed mixture alternately with water and buttermilk. Mix well.

◆ Fill paper-lined muffin cups two-thirds full. Bake at 375° for 12-15 minutes or until a toothpick comes out clean. Cool for 10 minutes before removing from pan to a wire rack to cool completely. Frost cupcakes.

YIELD: 16 SERVINGS.

MAPLE CARROT CUPCAKES

I come from a family of cooks and was inspired to cook and bake ever since I was young. This recipe is always requested at special gatherings.

—*Lisa Ann Panzino-DiNunzio, Vineland, New Jersey*

2	cups all-purpose flour
1	cup sugar
1	teaspoon baking powder
1	teaspoon baking soda
1	teaspoon ground cinnamon
1/2	teaspoon salt
4	eggs
1	cup canola oil
1/2	cup maple syrup
3	cups grated carrots (about 6 medium)

FROSTING:

1	package (8 ounces) cream cheese, softened
1/4	cup butter, softened
1/4	cup maple syrup
1	teaspoon vanilla extract

Chopped walnuts, optional

◆ In a large bowl, combine the first six ingredients. In another bowl, beat the eggs, oil and syrup. Stir into dry ingredients just until moistened. Fold in carrots.

◆ Fill greased or paper-lined muffin cups two-thirds full. Bake at 350° for 20-25 minutes or until a toothpick comes out clean. Cool for 5 minutes before removing cupcakes from pans to wire racks.

◆ For frosting, combine cream cheese, butter, syrup and vanilla in a bowl; beat until smooth. Frost cooled cupcakes. Sprinkle with nuts if desired.

YIELD: 18 SERVINGS.

PICNIC CUPCAKES

These tender cupcakes don't need frosting, so they're perfect for a picnic or traveling. Kids of all ages enjoy the delectable bites.

—*Forence Leinweber, Endicott, Washington*

1	package (18-1/2 ounces) chocolate *or* yellow cake mix

FILLING:

1	package (8 ounces) cream cheese, softened
1	egg, lightly beaten
1/3	cup sugar
1	cup (6 ounces) semisweet chocolate chips

◆ Mix cake according to package directions. Spoon batter into 24 greased or paper-lined muffin cups, filling two-thirds full. In a bowl, beat cream cheese, egg and sugar until smooth. Fold in the chips. Drop by tablespoonfuls into batter. Bake at 350° for 20 minutes or until cupcakes test done.

YIELD: 24 SERVINGS.

Traveling Cuppies

If you choose to frost your cupcakes, there are a few simple tricks to make transporting them a snap while protecting the frosting. A plastic cupcake carrier works well, or simply place the treats in an aluminun muffin pan and cover it with another muffin pan turned upside down. Secure the tins together with strong binder clips.

GERMAN CHOCOLATE CUPCAKES

These cupcakes disappear in a dash when I take them to the school where I teach. Pecans, coconut and brown sugar dress up the topping nicely.

—*Lettice Charmasson, San Diego, California*

1	package (18-1/4 ounces) German chocolate cake mix
1	cup water
3	eggs
1/2	cup canola oil
3	tablespoons chopped pecans
3	tablespoons flaked coconut
3	tablespoons brown sugar

◆ In a large bowl, combine the cake mix, water, eggs and oil. Beat on low speed for 30 seconds. Beat on medium speed for 2 minutes.

◆ Fill paper-lined muffin cups three-fourths full. Combine pecans, coconut and brown sugar; sprinkle over batter. Bake at 400° for 15-20 minutes or until a toothpick inserted in the center comes out clean. Cool for 10 minutes before removing from pans to wire racks to cool completely.

YIELD: 24 SERVINGS.

A Sticky Situation

When baking cupcakes or muffins in paper-lined muffin cups, spray the cups with cooking spray before filling them with the batter. Once baked, the liners peel off easily and leave no messy crumbs to clean up afterwards.

CHERRY CHEESE CUPCAKES

Our church Christmas party always includes these pretty cupcakes as my home-baked contribution. The holidays were the sweet inspiration for their cheery garnish of cherries and mint leaves.

—*Leanne Beagley, Rochester, New York*

3	packages (8 ounces *each*) cream cheese, softened
1-1/2	cups sugar, *divided*
1-1/2	teaspoons vanilla extract, *divided*
5	eggs
1	cup (8 ounces) sour cream
1-1/2	cups cherry pie filling

Mint leaves

◆ In a bowl, combine cream cheese, 1 cup sugar and 1 teaspoon vanilla; beat until smooth. Add eggs, one at a time, beating well after each addition.

◆ Spoon into foil-lined muffin cups. Bake at 300° for 25-30 minutes or until set. Cool 5 minutes.

◆ In a small bowl, combine sour cream and the remaining sugar and vanilla until smooth. Spoon onto cupcakes. Return to the oven for 6-8 minutes or until set. Cool completely.

◆ Top with pie filling. Garnish with mint leaves. Chill.

YIELD: 22-24 SERVINGS.

CAPPUCCINO CUPCAKES

If you're a java junkie, you'll fall for these enticing little treats. Add a dusting of cocoa powder to deliciously top off the cute bites.

—Carol Forcum, Marion, Illinois

2	cups all-purpose flour
1-1/2	cups sugar
1/2	cup baking cocoa
1	teaspoon baking soda
1/2	teaspoon salt
1/4	cup instant coffee granules
1/2	cup hot water
2	eggs
1/2	cup prune baby food
1/4	cup canola oil
2	teaspoons vanilla extract
1-1/2	cups reduced-fat whipped topping

Additional baking cocoa

◆ In a bowl, combine the flour, sugar, cocoa, baking soda and salt. Dissolve coffee granules in hot water. In a large bowl, whisk the eggs, baby food, oil, vanilla and coffee mixture. Gradually stir into dry ingredients just until moistened.

◆ Fill paper-lined muffin cups two-thirds full. Bake at 350° for 18-20 minutes or until a toothpick comes out clean. Cool for 10 minutes before removing from pans to wire racks to cool completely.

◆ Just before serving, frost cooled cupcakes with whipped topping and sprinkle with cocoa.

YIELD: 17 SERVINGS.

DOUBLE CHOCOLATE CUPCAKES

You don't have to skimp on chocolate to make a luscious treat without the extra calories. These moist cupcakes are chock-full of sweet flavor but low in saturated fat.

—Linda Utter, Sidney, Montana

2	tablespoons butter, softened
3/4	cup sugar
1	egg
1	egg white
1/2	cup plus 2 tablespoons buttermilk
1/3	cup water
1	tablespoon white vinegar
1	teaspoon vanilla extract
1-1/2	cups all-purpose flour
1/4	cup baking cocoa
1	teaspoon baking soda
1/2	teaspoon salt
1/3	cup miniature semisweet chocolate chips

◆ In a large bowl, cream butter and sugar until light and fluffy. Add egg and egg white, one at a time, beating well after each addition. Beat on high until light and fluffy. Stir in buttermilk, water, vinegar and vanilla. Combine the flour, cocoa, baking soda and salt; add to batter just until moistened. Stir in chocolate chips.

◆ Fill muffin cups coated with cooking spray three-fourths full. Bake at 375° for 15-18 minutes or until a toothpick comes out clean. Cool for 5 minutes before removing from pans to wire racks.

YIELD: 14 SERVINGS.

PEANUT BUTTER CUPCAKES

Peanut-butter lovers can double their pleasure with these tender treats. I use the popular ingredient in both the cupcakes and the creamy homemade frosting.
—*Ruth Hutson, Westfield, Indiana*

<table>
<tr><td>1/3</td><td>cup butter, softened</td></tr>
<tr><td>1/2</td><td>cup peanut butter</td></tr>
<tr><td>1-1/4</td><td>cups packed brown sugar</td></tr>
<tr><td>1</td><td>egg</td></tr>
<tr><td>1</td><td>teaspoon vanilla extract</td></tr>
<tr><td>2</td><td>cups all-purpose flour</td></tr>
<tr><td>2</td><td>teaspoons baking powder</td></tr>
<tr><td>1/2</td><td>teaspoon salt</td></tr>
<tr><td>1/4</td><td>teaspoon ground cinnamon</td></tr>
<tr><td>3/4</td><td>cup milk</td></tr>
</table>

FROSTING:

<table>
<tr><td>1/3</td><td>cup peanut butter</td></tr>
<tr><td>2</td><td>cups confectioners' sugar</td></tr>
<tr><td>2</td><td>teaspoons honey</td></tr>
<tr><td>1</td><td>teaspoon vanilla extract</td></tr>
<tr><td>3</td><td>to 4 tablespoons milk</td></tr>
</table>

◆ In a large bowl, cream the butter, peanut butter and brown sugar until light and fluffy. Beat in egg and vanilla. Combine the dry ingredients; add to creamed mixture alternately with milk and beat well after each addition.

◆ Fill paper-lined muffin cups two-thirds full. Bake at 350° for 26-30 minutes or until a toothpick comes out clean. Cool for 10 minutes before removing from pans to wire racks to cool completely.

◆ For frosting, in a small bowl, cream peanut butter and sugar until light and fluffy. Beat in honey and vanilla. Beat in enough milk to achieve a spreading consistency. Frost cupcakes.

YIELD: 18 SERVINGS.

Editor's Note: Reduced-fat or generic brands of peanut butter are not recommended for this recipe.

Batter Basics

Adding dry and wet ingredients alternately to batter prevents gluten from forming, which can make the texture tough. Begin by adding a third of the flour mixture and mix until the batter is smooth. Then add half of the milk, gently mixing until combined. Continue adding ingredients alternately, mixing the batter just until combined.

ST. PATRICK'S DAY CUPCAKES

These stir-and-bake cupcakes go together super quick. Pistachio pudding mix gives them a mild flavor and pretty pastel color that makes them perfect for St. Patrick's Day.
—*Kathy Meyer, Almond, Wisconsin*

<table>
<tr><td>1-3/4</td><td>cups all-purpose flour</td></tr>
<tr><td>2/3</td><td>cup sugar</td></tr>
<tr><td>1</td><td>package (3.4 ounces) instant pistachio pudding mix</td></tr>
<tr><td>2</td><td>teaspoons baking powder</td></tr>
<tr><td>1/2</td><td>teaspoon salt</td></tr>
<tr><td>2</td><td>eggs</td></tr>
<tr><td>1-1/4</td><td>cups milk</td></tr>
<tr><td>1/2</td><td>cup canola oil</td></tr>
<tr><td>1</td><td>teaspoon vanilla extract</td></tr>
</table>

Green food coloring, optional
Cream cheese frosting

◆ In a large bowl, combine the dry ingredients. In another bowl, beat eggs, milk, oil and vanilla; add to dry ingredients and mix until blended.

◆ Fill paper-lined muffin cups three-fourths full. Bake at 375° for 18-22 minutes or until a toothpick inserted in the center comes out clean. Cool on a wire rack. Add food coloring to frosting if desired. Frost cupcakes.

YIELD: 12 SERVINGS.

BROWNIE CUPS

These individual brownie-like cupcakes are studded with crunchy pecan pieces. The crinkly tops of these chewy treats are so pretty there's no need to add frosting.

—*Merrill Powers, Spearville, Kansas*

1	cup butter
1	cup (6 ounces) semisweet chocolate chips
1	cup chopped pecans
4	eggs
1-1/2	cups sugar
1	cup all-purpose flour
1	teaspoon vanilla extract

◆ In a small saucepan over low heat, melt the butter and chocolate chips, stirring until smooth. Cool. Add pecans; stir until well-coated. In a large bowl, combine the eggs, sugar, flour and vanilla extract. Fold in chocolate mixture.

◆ Fill paper-lined muffin cups two-thirds full. Bake at 325° for 35-38 minutes or until a toothpick inserted near the center comes out clean. Remove from pans to wire racks to cool.

YIELD: 18 SERVINGS.

CHOCOLATE MACAROON CUPCAKES

A delightful coconut and ricotta cheese filling is hidden inside these cupcakes. A light dusting of sweet confectioners' sugar adds the perfect finishing touch.

—*Dolores Skrout, Summerhill, Pennsylvania*

2	egg whites
1	egg
1/3	cup unsweetened applesauce
1	teaspoon vanilla extract
1-1/4	cups all-purpose flour
1	cup sugar
1/3	cup baking cocoa
1/2	teaspoon baking soda
3/4	cup buttermilk

FILLING:

1	cup fat-free ricotta cheese
1/4	cup sugar
1	egg white
1/3	cup flaked coconut
1/2	teaspoon coconut *or* almond extract
2	teaspoons confectioners' sugar

◆ In a bowl, combine the egg whites, egg, applesauce and vanilla. Combine the flour, sugar, cocoa and baking soda; gradually add to egg white mixture alternately with buttermilk. Spoon half of the batter into 18 muffin cups coated with cooking spray.

◆ In another bowl, beat the ricotta cheese, sugar and egg white until smooth. Stir in coconut and extract. Spoon 1 tablespoonful in the center of each muffin cup.

◆ Fill muffin cups two-thirds full with remaining batter. Bake at 350° for 28-33 minutes or until a toothpick inserted in cupcake comes out clean. Cool for 5 minutes before removing from pans to wire racks; cool completely. Dust with confectioners' sugar.

YIELD: 18 SERVINGS.

SPICE CUPCAKES

These moist, spicy cupcakes with creamy caramel frosting are a delicious treat. The recipe has been in my family for years. When I was growing up, the snacks were always in the freezer, just waiting to be snitched one at a time!
—*Carla Hodenfield, New Town, North Dakota*

2	cups water
1	cup raisins
1/2	cup shortening
1	cup sugar
1	egg
1-3/4	cups all-purpose flour
1	teaspoon baking soda
1/2	teaspoon salt
1/2	teaspoon *each* ground allspice, cloves, cinnamon and nutmeg
1/4	cup chopped walnuts

FROSTING:

1	cup packed brown sugar
1/3	cup half-and-half cream
1/4	teaspoon salt
3	tablespoons butter
1	teaspoon vanilla extract
1-1/4	cups confectioners' sugar

Coarsely chopped walnuts, optional

◆ In a large saucepan, bring water and raisins to a boil. Reduce heat; simmer for 10 minutes. Remove from heat and set aside (do not drain).

◆ Meanwhile, in a large bowl, cream shortening and sugar until light and fluffy. Beat in egg. Stir in raisins. Combine dry ingredients; add to creamed mixture until well blended. Stir in walnuts.

◆ Fill paper-lined muffin cups with 1/3 cup batter each. Bake at 350° for 20-25 minutes or until a toothpick comes out clean. Cool for 10 minutes; remove from pan to a wire rack.

◆ For frosting, in a large saucepan, combine brown sugar, cream and salt. Bring to a boil over medium-low heat; cook and stir until smooth. Stir in butter and vanilla. Remove from the heat; cool slightly. Stir in confectioners' sugar until smooth. Frost cupcakes; top with nuts if desired.

YIELD: 14 SERVINGS.

CREAM-FILLED CUPCAKES

These moist chocolate cupcakes have a fun filling and shiny chocolate frosting that make them different from any other. They always disappear in a flash.

—*Kathy Kittell, Lenexa, Kansas*

1	package (18-1/4 ounces) devil's food cake mix
2	teaspoons hot water
1/4	teaspoon salt
1	jar (7 ounce) marshmallow creme
1/2	cup shortening
1/3	cup confectioners' sugar
1/2	teaspoon vanilla extract

GANACHE FROSTING:

1	cup (6 ounces) semisweet chocolate chips
3/4	cup heavy whipping cream

◆ Prepare and bake cupcakes according to package directions for cupcakes. Cool for 5 minutes before removing to wire racks to cool completely.

◆ For filling, in a small bowl, combine water and salt until salt is dissolved. Cool. In a small bowl, beat the marshmallow creme, shortening, confectioners' sugar and vanilla until light and fluffy; add the salt mixture.

◆ Cut a small hole in the corner of pastry or plastic bag; insert round pastry tip. Fill the bag with cream filling. Push the tip through the bottom of paper liner to fill each cupcake.

◆ In a heavy saucepan, melt the chocolate chips with cream; stir until smooth. Cool. Dip cupcake tops into frosting; chill for 20 minutes or until set. Store in the refrigerator.

YIELD: 24 SERVINGS.

RASPBERRY SWIRL CUPCAKES

Prepared pie filling and an easy cake mix make these cupcakes a breeze to prepare. Dress them up with raspberries and mint for a pretty display.

—Christine Sohm, Newton, Ontario

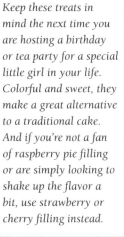
1   package (18-1/4 ounces) white cake mix
1/4 cup raspberry pie filling
1/2 cup shortening
1/3 cup milk
1   teaspoon vanilla extract
1/4 teaspoon salt
3   cups confectioners' sugar
Fresh raspberries and mint, optional

◆ Prepare and bake cake mix according to package directions. Fill paper-lined muffin cups two-thirds full. Drop 1/2 teaspoon of pie filling in the center of each; swirl with a knife.

◆ Bake at 350° for 20-25 minutes or until a toothpick inserted in the center comes out clean. Cool for 10 minutes before removing from pans to wire racks to cool completely.

◆ In a large bowl, beat shortening until fluffy. Add milk, vanilla, salt and confectioners' sugar; beat until smooth. Frost cupcakes. Garnish with raspberries and mint if desired.

YIELD: 18 SERVINGS.

APPLESAUCE SPICE CUPCAKES

I began making these tender cupcakes as a young girl and still enjoy baking them today. The flavors are the perfect blend of sugar and spice making them absolutely scrumptious.

—Edna Hoffman, Hebron, Indiana

1/3 cup butter, softened
3/4 cup sugar
2   eggs
1   teaspoon vanilla extract
1-1/3 cups all-purpose flour
1   teaspoon baking powder
1/2 teaspoon baking soda
1/2 teaspoon salt
1   teaspoon ground cinnamon
1/2 teaspoon ground nutmeg
1/8 teaspoon ground cloves
3/4 cup applesauce
Cream cheese frosting

◆ In a bowl, cream butter and sugar. Add eggs and vanilla; mix well. Combine dry ingredients; add to creamed mixture alternately with applesauce.

◆ Fill greased or paper-lined muffin cups two-thirds full. Bake at 350° for 25 minutes or until a toothpick inserted near the center comes out clean. Cool for 10 minutes before removing to a wire rack. Frost cooled cupcakes.

YIELD: 12 SERVINGS.

BANANA NUT CUPCAKES

These moist cupcakes taste like little loaves of banana bread. I keep ripe bananas in the freezer, so I can whip up these treats whenever I need them for a bake sale or party. I like to top them with cream cheese frosting.

—*Vicki Abrahamson, Silverdale, Washington*

1/3	cup butter-flavored shortening
2/3	cup sugar
2	eggs
1	cup mashed ripe bananas (about 3 medium)
2	tablespoons milk
1	tablespoon vanilla extract
1-1/3	cups all-purpose flour
2	teaspoons baking powder
1/2	teaspoon baking soda
1/4	teaspoon salt
1/4	cup chopped nuts

◆ In a large bowl, cream shortening and sugar until light and fluffy. Beat in the eggs. Stir in the bananas, milk and vanilla. Combine the flour, baking powder, baking soda and salt; gradually add to creamed mixture and mix well. Stir in nuts.

◆ Fill paper-lined muffin cups two-thirds full. Bake at 350° for 18-20 minutes or until a toothpick comes out clean. Cool for 5 minutes before removing from pans to wire racks.

YIELD: 15 SERVINGS.

Nutty Alternative

Countless baking recipes call for nuts of all kinds, but unfortunately many people are allergic to them. The next time you whip up a big batch of cupcakes or muffins, try substituting the nuts with crushed English toffee bits instead. The toffee pieces have a nice crunch and are a tasty addition sure to please.

ZUCCHINI CHIP CUPCAKES

My three girls love these nut-topped cupcakes even without frosting. This recipe is a great way to use up zucchini, and the treats freeze well for anytime snacking.

—*Debra Forshee, Stockton, Kansas*

1/2	cup butter, softened
1/2	cup oil
1-3/4	cups sugar
2	eggs
1/2	cup milk
1	teaspoon vanilla extract
2-1/2	cups all-purpose flour
1/4	cup baking cocoa
1	teaspoon baking soda
1/2	teaspoon salt
1/2	teaspoon ground cinnamon
2	cups shredded zucchini
1/4	cup miniature semisweet chocolate chips
1/4	cup chopped pecans

◆ In a large bowl, cream the butter, oil and sugar until light and fluffy. Beat in the eggs, milk and vanilla. Combine the flour, cocoa, baking soda, salt and cinnamon; gradually add to creamed mixture. Fold in the zucchini and chocolate chips.

◆ Fill greased or paper-lined muffin cups two-thirds full. Top with pecans. Bake at 375° for 20-25 minutes or until a toothpick inserted in center comes out clean. Cool for 10 minutes before removing from pans to wire racks to cool completely.

YIELD: 24 SERVINGS.

CHOCOLATE CARAMEL CUPCAKES

A few baking staples are all you need to throw together these chewy delights. Boxed cake mix and a can of frosting make them fast, but caramel, walnuts and chocolate chips tucked inside make them memorable. We like to serve them with a scoop of ice cream.

—Bev Spain, Belleville, Ohio

1   package (18-1/4 ounces) chocolate cake mix

24   caramels

3/4   cup semisweet chocolate chips

1   cup chopped walnuts

Chocolate frosting

Additional walnuts, optional

◆ Prepare cake mix batter according to package directions for cupcakes. Fill 24 paper-lined muffin cups one-third full; set remaining batter aside. Bake at 350° for 7-8 minutes or until top of cupcake appears set.

◆ Gently press a caramel into each cupcake; sprinkle with chocolate chips and walnuts. Top with remaining batter. Bake 15-20 minutes longer or until a toothpick comes out clean.

◆ Cool for 5 minutes before removing from pans to wire racks to cool completely. Frost cupcakes with chocolate frosting. Sprinkle with additional nuts if desired.

YIELD: 24 SERVINGS.

Cupcake Creations

IF YOU FALL for whimsical treats that are as much fun to create as they are to eat, then it's time to indulge your fancy! Whip up any one of the eye-catching works of art in this playful collection. From simple and cute to stylish and stunning, these dressed-up gems take the cake.

SURPRISE CUPCAKES, P. 35

FLOWERPOT CUPCAKES

These sweet treats are one of a number of "cooking club" projects at the after-school program I supervise. The flower-topped cupcakes are so easy that even children in our kindergarten make them. They're great for a spring or summer birthday party.

—*Jackie Hannahs, Fountain, Michigan*

> 1 package (18-1/4 ounces) devil's food cake mix
> 16 pieces Fruit by the Foot
> 24 large green gumdrops
> 48 large assorted gumdrops
> 48 pretzel sticks

◆ Prepare cake batter according to package directions for cupcakes. Fill paper-lined muffin cups two-thirds full.

◆ Bake at 350° for 18-20 minutes or until a toothpick comes out clean. Cool for 5 minutes; remove from pans to wire racks to cool completely.

◆ Cut three 9-in. pieces from each fruit roll piece (save small pieces for another use). With a small pastry brush, lightly brush water on one end of a fruit strip. Wrap around base of cupcake; press ends together. Repeat with remaining cupcakes. Lightly brush water on one side of remaining fruit strips; fold in half lengthwise. Brush one end with water; wrap around cupcake top, slightly overlapping bottom fruit strip.

◆ Press each gumdrop into a 1-1/4-in. circle. With scissors, cut each green gumdrop into four leaf shapes; set aside. Cut one end of each remaining gumdrop into a tulip shape. Gently press a pretzel into each tulip-shaped gumdrop. Gently press gumdrop leaves onto pretzels. Press two flowers into the top of each cupcake.

YIELD: 24 SERVINGS.

MINI BROWNIE TREATS

I like to take these simple goodies to potlucks and family gatherings. The sweet chocolate morsel atop each cupcake makes them impossible to resist.

—*Pam Kokes, North Loup, Nebraska*

> 1 package fudge brownie mix (13-inch x 9-inch pan size)
> 48 striped chocolate kisses

◆ Prepare brownie mix according to package directions for fudge-like brownies. Fill paper-lined miniature muffin cups two-thirds full.

◆ Bake at 350° for 18-21 minutes or until a toothpick comes out clean. Immediately top each with a chocolate kiss. Cool for 10 minutes before removing from pans to wire racks to cool completely.

YIELD: 48 SERVINGS.

POSY CUPCAKES

Our home economists suggest dressing up cupcakes from a mix with canned frosting and candied flowers. Don't want to fuss with perfectly placing the flowers? Crumble them for a fun confetti look.

—*Taste of Home Test Kitchen*

1 package (18-1/4 ounces) white *or* yellow cake mix

1 can (16 ounces) white *or* vanilla frosting

40 to 50 candied flowers

◆ Prepare cake batter according to package directions.

◆ Fill greased, foil or paper-lined muffin cups two-thirds full. Bake at 350° for 18-24 minutes or until a toothpick comes out clean. Cool for 5 minutes before removing from pans to wire racks to cool completely. Frost cupcakes. Decorate with candied flowers.

YIELD: 24 SERVINGS.

Editor's Note: Verify that candied flowers are edible and have not been treated with chemicals.

PUMPKIN CHIP CUPCAKES

I love these cupcakes loaded with chocolate chips and chopped walnuts. My mom makes them for dessert on special occasions or for delicious snacks.

—Jacinta Ransom, South Haven, Michigan

1	cup all-purpose flour
3/4	cup whole wheat flour
1	teaspoon baking powder
1	teaspoon baking soda
1/2	teaspoon salt
1/2	teaspoon ground cinnamon
1/4	teaspoon ground nutmeg
2	eggs, lightly beaten
1	cup canned pumpkin
1/2	cup canola oil
1/2	cup honey
1/3	cup water
1/2	cup chopped walnuts
1	cup miniature chocolate chips

FROSTING:

1	package (8 ounces) cream cheese, softened
1/4	cup butter, softened
1	teaspoon vanilla extract
2	cups confectioners' sugar

◆ In a large bowl, combine the first seven ingredients. Combine the eggs, pumpkin, oil, honey and water; mix well. Stir into dry ingredients just until combined; fold in walnuts and chocolate chips.

◆ Fill greased or foil-lined muffin cups three-fourths full. Bake at 350° for 20-25 minutes or until a toothpick comes out clean. Cool for 10 minutes before removing from pans to wire racks to cool completely.

◆ For frosting, in a small bowl, beat the cream cheese, butter and vanilla extract until fluffy. Gradually beat in confectioners' sugar until smooth. Frost cooled cupcakes.

YIELD: 15 SERVINGS.

APPLE SPICE CUPCAKES

A spice cake mix makes these moist confections a snap to stir up and a fast frosting helps them stand out from an orchard of goodies. They're super sellers at bake sales, too.

—Taste of Home Test Kitchen

> 1 package (18-1/4 ounces) spice cake mix
> 1-1/4 cups water
> 3 eggs
> 1/3 cup applesauce
>
> FROSTING:
>
> 1 package (8 ounces) cream cheese, softened
> 1/4 cup butter, softened
> 1 teaspoon vanilla extract
> 4 cups confectioners' sugar
>
> Red paste *or* liquid food coloring
>
> 24 pieces black licorice (3/4 inch)
> 12 green spice gumdrops

◆ In a large bowl, beat the cake mix, water, eggs and applesauce on low speed for 30 seconds. Beat on medium for 2 minutes.

◆ Fill paper-lined muffin cups two-thirds full. Bake at 350° for 18-22 minutes or until a toothpick inserted in the center comes out clean. Cool for 10 minutes before removing from pans to wire racks to cool completely.

◆ In a small bowl, beat the cream cheese, butter and vanilla until fluffy. Gradually add sugar, beating until smooth. Stir in food coloring.

◆ Frost tops of cupcakes. Insert licorice into centers for apple stems. Cut gumdrops in half; flatten and pinch to form leaves. Place one leaf next to each stem.

YIELD: 24 SERVINGS.

BERRY SURPRISE CUPCAKES

Tasty fruit rolls and chewy fruit snacks add a burst of flavor to these simple white cupcakes. Add them to kids' lunches for a sweet afternoon treat.

—Susan Lucas, Brampton, Ontario

> 1 package (18-1/4 ounces) white cake mix
> 1-1/3 cups water
> 3 egg whites
> 2 tablespoons canola oil
> 3 strawberry Fruit Roll-Ups, unrolled
> 1 can (16 ounces) vanilla frosting
> 6 pouches strawberry Fruit Snacks

◆ In a large bowl, combine the cake mix, water, eggs whites and oil. Beat on low speed for 30 seconds. Beat on medium for 2 minutes. Fill paper-lined muffin cups half full. Cut each fruit roll into eight pieces; place one piece over batter in each cup. Fill two-thirds full with remaining batter.

◆ Bake at 350° for 15-20 minutes or until a toothpick comes out clean. Cool for 10 minutes before removing from pans to wire racks to cool completely. Frost with vanilla frosting; decorate with fruit snacks.

YIELD: 24 SERVINGS.

Editor's Note: This recipe was tested with Betty Crocker Fruit Roll-Ups and Nabisco Fruit Snacks.

Surprise, Surprise!

Who doesn't like a sweet surprise in the center of a fluffy cupcake? Chewy fruit snacks are just one of many fun ingredients to add. For a new flavor twist, try jam, preserves, a peanut butter cup, a chocolate kiss, fruity pie filling, caramels, cream cheese, coconut flakes or a homemade cream made from shortening.

RUDOLPH CUPCAKES

These fast creations are perfect for occasions when you have to whip up a batch of treats for a school party. With no ready-made decorations on hand, I created these red-nosed cakes in a jiffy by sticking animal crackers in the cupcakes for antlers and used other sweets for the eyes and noses. They're easy enough for children to help with, too.

—*Karen Gardiner, Eutaw, Alabama*

1	package (18-1/4 ounces) cake mix of your choice
1	can (16 ounces) chocolate frosting
48	animal crackers
24	miniature marshmallows, halved
48	miniature chocolate chips *or* raisins
24	red jelly beans

◆ Prepare and bake cake mix according to package directions for cupcakes, using foil or paper-lined muffin cups. Cool cupcakes for 10 minutes before removing from pans to wire racks to cool completely.

◆ Frost cupcake tops. Insert two animal crackers into each cupcake for antlers. For the eyes, place two marshmallow halves, cut side up, with a chocolate chip in the center of each. Add a jelly bean for nose.

YIELD: 24 SERVINGS.

SANTA CUPCAKES

My kids leave out at least one cupcake for Santa on Christmas Eve. These jolly confections are always a hit with ol' Saint Nick!

—*Sharon Skildum, Maple Grove, Minnesota*

1	package (18-1/4 ounces) white cake mix
1	can (16 ounces) *or* 2 cups vanilla frosting, *divided*

Red gel *or* paste food coloring

Miniature marshmallows, chocolate chips, red-hot candies and flaked coconut

◆ Prepare and bake cake mix according to package directions for cupcakes. Cool for 10 minutes; remove from pans to wire racks to cool completely.

◆ Place 2/3 cup frosting in a small bowl; tint with red food coloring. Set aside 3 tablespoons white frosting for decorating. Cover two-thirds of the top of each cupcake with remaining white frosting. Frost remaining one-third of tops with red frosting for hat.

◆ Place reserved white frosting in a small heavy-duty resealable plastic bag; cut a 1/4-in. hole in one corner. On each cupcake, pipe a line of frosting to create fur band of hat.

◆ Press a marshmallow on one side of hat for pom-pom. Under hat, place two chocolate chips for eyes and one red-hot candy for nose. Gently press coconut onto face for beard.

YIELD: 18 SERVINGS.

CUPCAKES WITH WHIPPED CREAM FROSTING

While not as sweet as buttercream, this frosting made with whipping cream is smooth, creamy and a pleasure to pipe onto cupcakes.

—Taste of Home Test Kitchen

1	package (18-1/4 ounces) white cake mix
1-1/4	teaspoons unflavored gelatin
5	teaspoons cold water
1-1/4	cups heavy whipping cream
5	tablespoons confectioners' sugar
1/4	teaspoon vanilla extract

Red and yellow food coloring

◆ Prepare and bake cake mix according to package directions for cupcakes. Cool on wire racks.

◆ In a small saucepan, sprinkle gelatin over water; let stand for 1 minute to soften. Heat over low heat, stirring until gelatin is completely dissolved. Remove from the heat; cool.

◆ In a large bowl, beat whipping cream until it begins to thicken. Add the sugar, vanilla and gelatin mixture; beat until soft peaks form. Set aside 1 cup for decorating.

◆ Spread remaining frosting over tops of cupcakes. Divide reserved frosting in half; tint one portion pink and the other yellow.

◆ Use a toothpick to outline the shape of heart, flower or sunburst on tops of cupcakes. Use a medium star tip to pipe pink or yellow stars along outline. Fill in the shape with piped stars as desired.

YIELD: 24 SERVINGS.

BERRY-TOPPED WHITE CUPCAKES

Guests love these yummy white cupcakes topped with a cream cheese frosting. The strawberry-blueberry garnish makes them the perfect treat for a patriotic-themed party on Memorial Day or the Fourth of July.

—Judy Kenninger, Brownsburg, Indiana

5 egg whites

1/2 cup plus 2 tablespoons butter, softened

1 cup sugar, *divided*

3/4 teaspoon vanilla extract

2-1/4 cups cake flour

2-1/4 teaspoons baking powder

1/2 teaspoon salt

3/4 cup milk

ICING:

4 ounces cream cheese, softened

1/3 cup butter, softened

2 cups confectioners' sugar

1/2 teaspoon lemon juice

Fresh berries *or* fruit of your choice

◆ Place egg whites in a large bowl; let stand at room temperature for 30 minutes. In another bowl, cream butter and 3/4 cup sugar until light and fluffy. Beat in vanilla extract. Combine the flour, baking powder and salt; add to creamed mixture alternately with milk.

◆ Beat egg whites on medium speed until soft peaks form. Gradually beat in remaining sugar, about 2 tablespoons at a time, on high until stiff, glossy peaks form and sugar is dissolved. Fold one-fourth of the egg whites into batter; fold in remaining egg whites.

◆ With a spoon, gently fill foil- or paper-lined muffin cups two-thirds full. Bake at 350° for 18-22 minutes. Cool cupcakes for 10 minutes before removing from pans to wire racks to cool completely.

◆ For icing, in a small bowl, beat cream cheese and butter until smooth. Gradually beat in confectioners' sugar and lemon juice. Spread over cupcakes. Top with fruit.

YIELD: 22 SERVINGS.

CUPCAKE CONES

Kids of all ages love these charming cupcake cones perfect for picnics and backyard barbeques. The cream cheese filling in the center adds a sweet surprise.

—*Betty Anderson, Sturgeon Bay, Wisconsin*

1 package (18-1/4 ounces) chocolate cake mix
1 package (8 ounces) cream cheese, softened
1/3 cup sugar
1 egg
1/2 teaspoon vanilla extract
1 cup miniature semisweet chocolate chips
36 ice-cream cake cones (about 3 inches tall)

FROSTING:

1/2 cup shortening
3-3/4 cups confectioners' sugar
1 teaspoon vanilla extract
4 to 5 tablespoons milk

◆ Prepare cake mix according to package directions; set aside.

◆ In a bowl, beat the cream cheese, sugar, egg and vanilla until smooth; stir in chocolate chips. Place ice-cream cones in muffin cups. Spoon about 1 tablespoon of cake batter into each cone; top with a rounded teaspoon of cream cheese mixture. Fill with remaining batter to within 3/4 in. of top. Bake at 350° for 25-30 minutes or until a toothpick comes out clean.

◆ In a bowl, beat the shortening, confectioners' sugar and vanilla. Add enough milk to achieve spreading consistency. Frost tops of cooled cones.

YIELD: 36 SERVINGS.

Editor's Note: These cupcakes are best served the day they are made.

CARROT-TOPPED CUPCAKES

A handy spice cake mix gets a tasty treatment when dressed up with shredded carrots and chopped walnuts. The mini carrot cakes are eye-catching, too, when decorated with carrots piped on with prepared cream cheese frosting and parsley sprigs for the green tops.

—*Taste of Home Test Kitchen*

1 package (18-1/4 ounces) spice cake mix
1-1/2 cups shredded carrots
1/2 cup chopped walnuts
1 teaspoon ground cinnamon
1 can (16 ounces) cream cheese frosting
Orange paste food coloring
Fresh parsley sprigs

◆ Prepare cake batter according to package directions. Fold in carrots, walnuts and cinnamon.

◆ Fill paper-lined muffin cups half full. Bake at 350° for 18-23 minutes or until a toothpick comes out clean. Remove from pans to wire racks to cool completely.

◆ Frost cupcakes with 1-1/4 cups frosting. Place remaining frosting in a small resealable plastic bag; tint with orange food coloring. Cut a small hole in the corner of bag; pipe a carrot on the top of each cupcake. Add a parsley sprig for greens.

YIELD: 24 SERVINGS.

CANDIED HOLLY CUPCAKES

My mother often made these fruity spice cupcakes. Decorated with cherries and citron, they add a festive touch to the holidays.

—Pam Goodlet, Washington Island, Wisconsin

1/2	cup shortening
1	cup sugar
2	eggs
1-1/2	cups all-purpose flour
1/2	teaspoon baking soda
1/2	teaspoon *each* ground cinnamon, allspice, nutmeg and cloves
1/2	cup buttermilk
1/2	cup cherry jam *or* flavor of your choice
1/2	cup chopped pecans
1/4	cup finely chopped candied cherries
1/4	cup finely chopped candied orange peel
2	cups prepared vanilla frosting
9	candied cherries, halved
18	green citron pieces *or* green candied pineapple pieces, cut into strips

◆ In a large bowl, cream shortening and sugar until light and fluffy. Beat in eggs. Combine the flour, baking soda and spices; add to creamed mixture alternately with buttermilk, beating well after each addition. Stir in the jam, pecans, cherries and orange peel.

◆ Fill paper-lined muffin cups three-fourths full. Bake at 350° for 20-25 minutes or until a toothpick comes out clean. Cool for 10 minutes before removing from pans to wire racks to cool completely.

◆ Frost cooled cupcakes. Decorate with candied cherries for holly berries and citron for leaves.

YIELD: 18 SERVINGS.

SCAREDY CAKES

Our home economists guarantee kids of all ages will delight in these funny-faced cupcakes. You can even enlist your little ones to help decorate them, using the candies we suggest or other candies to suit your taste.

—Taste of Home Test Kitchen

1	package (18-1/4 ounces) yellow cake mix
1	can (16 ounces) vanilla frosting

Green gel food coloring, optional

Assorted candies of your choice (Chiclets, black licorice nips, red shoestring licorice, Gummi Worms, M&M's, Life Savers, gumballs, strawberry sour belts, Tart & Tangy's, Tic Tacs)

◆ Prepare and bake cake according to package directions for cupcakes. Cool for 5 minutes before removing from pans to wire racks to cool completely.

◆ Tint some of the frosting green if desired. Frost cupcakes. Decorate with assorted colored candies to create monster faces.

YIELD: 24 SERVINGS.

SURPRISE CUPCAKES

My mother taught me this simple way to fill cupcakes with fruit jelly. Take these tender treats to your next get-together and watch faces light up after just one bite.
—*Edith Holliday, Flushing, Michigan*

1	cup shortening
2	cups sugar
2	eggs
2	teaspoons vanilla extract
3-1/2	cups all-purpose flour
5	teaspoons baking powder
1	teaspoon salt
1-1/2	cups milk
3/4	cup strawberry *or* grape jelly

Frosting of your choice

Colored sprinkles, optional

◆ In a large bowl, cream shortening and sugar. Add eggs, one at a time, beating well after each addition. Beat in vanilla. Combine the flour, baking powder and salt; add to creamed mixture alternately with milk, beating well after each addition.

◆ Fill 36 paper-lined muffin cups half full. Spoon 1 teaspoon jelly in the center of each. Bake at 375° for 15-20 minutes or until a toothpick inserted 1 in. from the edge comes out clean. Cool for 5 minutes; remove from pans to wire racks to cool completely. Frost and decorate with sprinkles if desired.

YIELD: 36 SERVINGS.

BUNNY CUPCAKES

Celebrate spring with these yummy cupcakes created from a simple cake mix, frosting and marshmallows. Cookies form the ears while candy gives these cute critters their funny faces.

—Taste of Home Test Kitchen

> 1 package (18-1/4 ounces) yellow cake mix
> 1 can (16 ounces) cream cheese frosting, *divided*
> 8 drops green food coloring
> 12 large marshmallows
> 3/4 cup flaked coconut, chopped
> 24 miniature pink jelly beans
> 12 miniature red jelly beans
> 24 miniature white jelly beans

Red shoestring licorice

> 1 to 2 drops red food coloring
> 48 small oval sugar cookies

◆ Prepare and bake cupcake according to package directions for cupcakes. Cool on wire racks.

◆ In a small bowl, combine 1 cup frosting and green food coloring; frost cupcake. Set remaining frosting aside. Cut marshmallows in half; immediately dip cut ends into coconut. Place coconut side up on cupcakes to form heads.

◆ Cut pink and red jelly beans in half widthwise. Cut white jelly beans in half lengthwise. With a toothpick, dab reserved frosting onto cut sides of pink jelly bean halves; attach to marshmallows for eyes. Attach red jelly beans for noses and white jelly beans for teeth.

◆ For whiskers, cut licorice into 1-in. pieces; attach four pieces to each cupcake. Tint remaining frosting pink. Cut a small hole in corner of a resealable plastic bag; add pink frosting. For ears, pipe an oval outline toward center of each cookie; insert two ears into each cupcake.

YIELD: 24 SERVINGS.

KITTY CAT CUPCAKES

On a bake sale table or alone at home, these feline treats won't last nine lives! The cute candy faces will catch attention fast...and the tasty orange-coconut cake will have folks snatching seconds.

—Doris Barb, El Dorado, Kansas

2/3	cup shortening
1-3/4	cups sugar, *divided*
4	eggs, *separated*
2-1/2	cups all-purpose flour
2-1/2	teaspoons baking powder
1/2	teaspoon salt
1	cup orange juice
1	cup flaked coconut

FROSTING:

1-1/4	cups sugar
1/4	cup water
1/4	cup light corn syrup
1	egg white
1/8	teaspoon salt
1/2	cup miniature marshmallows (about 50)
1/2	teaspoons vanilla extract

Assorted M&M's

1	piece red shoestring licorice, cut into 3/4-inch pieces

Chocolate sprinkles

About 9 vanilla wafers

2	cups flaked coconut, toasted

Let eggs stand at room temperature for 30 minutes. In a large bowl, cream shortening and 1-1/2 cups sugar until light and fluffy. Beat in egg yolks until well blended. Combine the flour, baking powder and salt; add to creamed mixture alternately with orange juice, beating well after each addition.

In a small bowl and with clean beaters, beat egg whites until soft peaks form. Continue beating on high; gradually add the remaining sugar, 1 tablespoon at a time, until stiff peaks form. Gradually fold into batter with coconut.

Fill paper-lined muffin cups two-thirds full. Bake at 350° for 15 minutes or until a toothpick comes out clean. Cool for 10 minutes before removing cupcakes from pans to the wire racks to cool completely.

For frosting, in a heavy saucepan, combine the sugar, water, corn syrup, egg white and salt. With a portable mixer, beat on low speed for 1 minute. Continue beating on low over low heat until frosting reaches 160°, about 12-18 minutes. Pour into a large bowl; add marshmallows and vanilla. Beat on high until stiff peaks form, about 5 minutes. Frost cupcakes.

Arrange M&M's for eyes and nose, licorice for mouth and sprinkles for whiskers. For ears, cut wafers into quarters with a serrated knife; place two on each cupcake, rounded side down. Sprinkle with coconut. Refrigerate until serving.

YIELD: 18 SERVINGS.

Editor's Note: A stand mixer is recommended for beating the frosting after it reaches 160°.

All Dressed Up

Looking for a quick way to dress up cupcakes? Try this easy layering technique. Prepare both chocolate and white cake batter. Fill paper-lined muffin cups with a large spoonful of chocolate batter into each. Gently add some white batter over the chocolate. Top with another spoonful of chocolate, being careful not to overfill the cups.

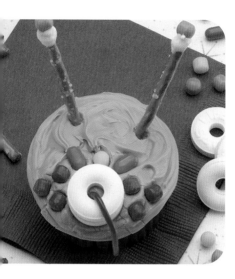

OUT-OF-THIS-WORLD CUPCAKES

These are a cinch to bake and even more fun to decorate! Our home economists turned out a pair of not-so-scary aliens, but you can let your imagination run wild and create critters, princesses, trains...the sky's the limit. Or save the decorating fun for a party activity, and let the kids top their cakes any way they want.
—*Taste of Home Test Kitchen*

1 package (18-1/4 ounces) yellow cake mix
1 can (16 ounces) vanilla frosting
Green gel food coloring *or* color of your choice, optional
Pretzel ticks, Tic Tacs, Life Savers, red string licorice, Tart & Tinys, Chuckles, and Peanut M&M's *or* candies of your choice

◆ Prepare cake mix batter according to package directions for cupcakes.

◆ Fill greased or paper-lined muffin cups two-thirds full. Bake at 350° for 18-24 minutes or until a toothpick comes out clean. Cool for 5 minutes before removing from pans to wire racks to cool completely.

◆ Tint the frosting with food coloring if desired. Frost cupcakes and decorate as desired.

YIELD: 24 SERVINGS.

CONVERSATION CUPCAKES

It's a snap to spell out sweet sentiments on these quaint cupcakes when you bake a batch ahead of time. You don't even need a heart-shaped muffin tin to make them.
—*Taste of Home Test Kitchen*

1 package (18-1/4 ounces) white cake mix
4 cups confectioners' sugar
1/2 cup butter, softened
1/2 cup shortening
1 teaspoon vanilla extract
1/8 teaspoon butter flavoring, optional
2 tablespoons milk
1 to 2 drops red food coloring, optional
1 to 2 drops yellow food coloring, optional
1 to 2 drops blue food coloring, optional

◆ Prepare cake mix batter according to package directions for cupcakes.

◆ Place paper or foil liners in a heart-shaped or standard muffin tin. Fill cups half full of batter. Bake according to package directions for cupcakes. Cool for 10 minutes; remove from pans to wire racks to cool completely.

◆ For frosting, in a large bowl, combine the confectioners' sugar, butter, shortening, vanilla, butter flavoring if desired and milk until smooth.

◆ Divide frosting into fourths if desired; place in four separate bowls. Leave one bowl untinted. Add one color of food coloring to each of the other three bowls; stir until well blended. Frost cupcakes. Pipe untinted frosting around edges and decorate tops with seasonal words or phrases.

YIELD: 28 SERVINGS.

ST. PATTY'S DAY CUPCAKES

On St. Patrick's Day our family gets together for a special dinner and other festivities. Green is dominant in most of the food we serve, so these cupcakes tinted with pistachio pudding mix are a perfect addition.

—Susan Frantz, Pittsburgh, Pennsylvania

1-3/4 cups all-purpose flour
  2/3 cup sugar
    1 package (3.4 ounces) instant pistachio pudding mix
2-1/2 teaspoons baking powder
  1/2 teaspoon salt
    2 eggs
1-1/2 cups milk
  1/2 cup canola oil
    1 teaspoon vanilla extract
  3/4 cup miniature semisweet chocolate chips
    1 cup cream cheese frosting
Green sprinkles *and/or* chocolate jimmies

◆ In a large bowl, combine the flour, sugar, pudding mix, baking powder and salt. In another bowl, combine the eggs, milk, oil and vanilla. Stir into dry ingredients until combined. Fold in chocolate chips.

◆ Fill foil or paper-lined muffin cups two-thirds full. Bake at 375° for 18-20 minutes or until a toothpick comes out clean. Cool for 5 minutes before removing from pans to wire racks to cool completely. Frost and decorate as desired.

YIELD: 18 SERVINGS.

CREEPY CUPCAKES

Our home economists put a Halloween spin on these no-fuss delights. With chocolate bodies and licorice legs, these spiders on cobwebs will "catch" everyone's attention!
—Taste of Home Test Kitchen

- 1 package (18-1/4 ounces) devil's food cake mix
- 1/4 cup butter, softened
- 1 package (3 ounces) cream cheese, softened
- 3 cups confectioners' sugar
- 2 tablespoons plus 1 teaspoon milk, *divided*
- 1/2 teaspoon vanilla extract

Red and yellow liquid food coloring *or* orange paste food coloring

- 1 tablespoon baking cocoa

Round pastry tip #3

- 9 chocolate kisses
- 9 semisweet chocolate chips

Black shoestring licorice, cut into 3/4-inch pieces

- 18 white nonpareils

- Prepare cake mix batter according to package directions.

- Fill greased jumbo muffin cups with 1/2 cup batter. Bake at 350° for 25-30 minutes or until a toothpick comes out clean. Cool for 5 minutes before removing from pans to wire racks to cool completely. Cut a thin slice off the top of each cupcake.

- In a bowl, cream butter, cream cheese, confectioners' sugar, 2 tablespoons milk and vanilla; mix well. Remove 1 cup; tint orange and frost cupcakes. To the remaining frosting, add baking cocoa and remaining milk. Cut a small hole in the corner of a pastry or plastic bag; insert round tip. Fill with chocolate frosting. Pipe a web on each cupcake; set remaining frosting aside.

- For spider, insert chocolate kiss, point side down, next to edge of cupcake. Insert chocolate chip, point side down, next to kiss. Place four licorice pieces on each side of kiss. For eyes, pipe two small circles of chocolate frosting on chocolate chip; insert nonpareils.

YIELD: 9 SERVINGS.

CHOCOLATE CREAM-FILLED CUPCAKES

Folks who enjoy homemade chocolate cupcakes are even more impressed when they bite into these treats and find a fluffy cream filling. These are great in a lunch box or on a buffet table.

—*Edie DeSpain, Logan, Utah*

2	cups sugar
1	cup milk
1	cup canola oil
1	cup water
2	eggs
1	teaspoon vanilla extract
3	cups all-purpose flour
1/3	cup baking cocoa
2	teaspoons baking soda
1	teaspoon salt

FILLING:

1/4	cup butter, softened
1/4	cup shortening
2	cups confectioners' sugar
3	tablespoons milk
1	teaspoon vanilla extract

Pinch salt

Chocolate frosting

In a large bowl, beat the sugar, milk, oil, water, eggs and vanilla until well blended. Combine the flour, cocoa, baking soda and salt; gradually beat into egg mixture until blended.

Fill paper-lined muffin cups half full. Bake at 375° for 15-20 minutes or until a toothpick inserted near the center comes out clean. Remove from pans to wire racks to cool completely.

In a small bowl, beat the butter, shortening, confectioners' sugar, milk, vanilla and salt until fluffy, about 5 minutes. Insert a very small tip into a pastry or plastic bag; fill with cream filling. Push the tip through the bottom of paper liner to fill each cupcake. Frost cupcakes.

YIELD: 36 SERVINGS.

CANDY CORN CUPCAKES

These moist, tender white cupcakes are perfect for any occasion. For fast yet fabulous results any time of year, choose candy decorations appropriate to the season.

—*Renee Schwebach, Dumont, Minnesota*

1/2	cup shortening
1-1/2	cups sugar
1	teaspoon vanilla extract
2	cups all-purpose flour
3-1/2	teaspoons baking powder
1	teaspoon salt
1	cup milk
4	egg whites

Frosting of your choice

Candy corn *or other decorations*

In a large bowl, cream shortening and sugar until light and fluffy. Beat in

vanilla. Combine the flour, baking powder and salt; add to the creamed mixture alternately with milk, beating well after each addition. Beat in the egg whites.

Fill paper-lined muffin cups half full. Bake at 350° for 18-22 minutes or until toothpick inserted near the center comes out clean. Cool for 10 minutes before removing from pans to wire racks to cool completely. Frost cooled cupcakes; decorate as desired.

YIELD: 24 SERVINGS.

STRAWBERRY MUFFIN CONES

This is a delightful way to serve nutritious muffins. Youngsters love the "ice cream cone" look and ease of eating. Adults say snacking on these cones makes them feel like kids again.

—*Barb Kietzer, Niles, Michigan*

2	cups all-purpose flour
1/2	cup sugar
2	teaspoons baking powder
1/2	teaspoon baking soda
1/2	teaspoon salt
2	eggs
1	carton (6 ounces) strawberry yogurt
1/2	cup canola oil
1	cup chopped fresh strawberries
15	ice cream cake cones (about 3 inches tall)
1	cup (6 ounces) semisweet chocolate chips
1	tablespoon shortening

Colored sprinkles

◆ In a large bowl, combine the first five ingredients. In another bowl, beat the eggs, yogurt, oil and strawberries; stir mixture into the dry ingredients just until moistened.

◆ Place the ice cream cones in muffin cups; spoon about 3 tablespoons batter into each cone. Bake at 375° for 19-21 minutes or until a toothpick inserted near the center comes out clean. Cool cones completely.

◆ In a saucepan over low heat, melt chocolate chips and shortening; stir until smooth. Dip muffin tops in chocolate; decorate with sprinkles.

YIELD: 15 SERVINGS.

BLACK CAT CUPCAKES

If a black cat crosses your path, we hope it's one of these chocolaty creations. This time-saving recipe relies on a boxed cake mix and a can of prepared frosting jazzed up with simple cookie and candy decorations.

—*Taste of Home Test Kitchen*

1	package (18-1/4 ounces) chocolate cake mix
1	can (16 ounces) dark chocolate frosting
12	chocolate cream-filled sandwich cookies, quartered
48	yellow jelly beans
24	black jelly beans
24	pieces black rope licorice

◆ Prepare and bake cake mix according to package directions for cupcakes, filling paper-lined muffin cups two-thirds full. Cool for 10 minutes before removing from pans to wire racks to cool completely.

◆ Frost tops of cupcakes. Insert two cookie pieces into each for ears. Add yellow jelly beans for eyes and a black jelly bean for nose. Cut each piece of licorice into thirds, then in half; place three licorice halves on each side of nose for whiskers.

YIELD: 24 SERVINGS.

CUPCAKE EASTER BASKETS

These dressed-up Easter cupcakes have a mild orange flavor. Our kids loved to help in the fun of decorating these blissful treats every spring.

—Julie Johnston, Shaunavon, Saskatchewan

1/2	cup butter, softened
1	cup sugar
1	egg
1	teaspoon grated orange peel
2	cups cake flour
3/4	teaspoon baking soda
1/2	teaspoon baking powder
1/4	teaspoon salt
2/3	cup buttermilk

FROSTING:

3/4	cup butter, softened
2	packages (3 ounces *each*) cream cheese, softened
1	teaspoon vanilla extract
3	cups confectioners' sugar
1	teaspoon water
4	drops green food coloring
1-1/2	cups flaked coconut

Red shoestring licorice

Jelly beans

◆ In a large bowl, cream butter and sugar. Beat in the egg and orange peel. Combine the flour, baking soda, baking powder and salt; add dry ingredients to the creamed mixture alternately with buttermilk.

◆ Fill paper-lined muffin cups two-thirds full. Bake at 350° for 20-25 minutes or until a toothpick comes out clean. Cool for 10 minutes before removing from pans to wire racks to cool completely.

◆ In a small bowl, beat butter, cream cheese and vanilla until smooth. Gradually beat in confectioners' sugar; spread over cupcakes. Combine water and food coloring in a large resealable plastic bag; add coconut. Seal bag and shake to tint. Sprinkle over cupcakes.

◆ Using a metal or wooden skewer, poke a hole in the top on opposite sides of each cupcake. Cut licorice into 6-in. strips for handle; insert each end into a hole. Decorate with jelly beans.

YIELD: 18 SERVINGS.

Muffins

TENDER, WARM and impossible to resist, there's nothing better than a big batch of muffins to show how much you care. The from-scratch baked goodness you'll find here is sure to have mouths watering with sweet anticipation.

APPLE STREUSEL MUFFINS, P. 49

MOM'S MUFFINS

These muffins were always a special treat when I was a child. Now I have lots of muffin recipes, and I make one kind or another several times each week. But none are better than these...and, for me, none come out of the oven with so many heartwarming memories attached!

—Jane Jensen, Yuma, Arizona

- 2 cups all-purpose flour
- 2 tablespoons plus 1 teaspoon sugar
- 4 teaspoons baking powder
- 1 teaspoon salt
- 2 eggs, beaten
- 3/4 cup milk
- 1/4 cup canola oil

◆ In a bowl, combine the flour, sugar, baking powder and salt. Make a well in the center. Combine the eggs, milk and oil. Pour into well and mix just until dry ingredients are moistened (do not overmix).

◆ Spoon into greased muffin cups. Bake at 400° for 20-25 minutes or until golden brown.

YIELD: 12 SERVINGS.

RASPBERRY BUTTERMILK MUFFINS

Classic buttermilk muffins get a twist with raspberries and chopped nuts. The light sprinkling of sugar on top gives them a sweet crunch too good to resist.

—Dawn Wright, Moline, Michigan

- 2 cups all-purpose flour
- 3/4 cup sugar
- 1/4 cup buttermilk blend powder
- 2-1/2 teaspoons baking powder
- 1/2 teaspoon baking soda
- 1 egg, lightly beaten
- 1 cup milk
- 1/3 cup canola oil
- 1 teaspoon lemon juice
- 1 cup fresh raspberries
- 1/2 cup chopped nuts

Additional sugar

◆ In a large bowl, combine the first five ingredients. Combine the egg, milk, oil and lemon juice; mix well. Stir into dry ingredients just until moistened. Fold in raspberries and nuts.

◆ Fill greased or paper-lined muffin cups three-fourths full. Sprinkle with sugar. Bake at 400° for 18-20 minutes or until muffins test done. Cool in pan for 5 minutes before removing to a wire rack to cool completely.

YIELD: 12 SERVINGS.

Editor's Note: 1 cup buttermilk can be substituted for the buttermilk blend powder; omit the 1 cup of milk.

BLUEBERRY STREUSEL MUFFINS

What a joy to set out a basket of these moist blueberry muffins topped with a super streusel on the brunch buffet. People rave when they taste them for the first time.
—Mary Anne McWhirter, Pearland, Texas

1/4	cup butter, softened
1/3	cup sugar
1	egg, beaten
1	teaspoon vanilla extract
2-1/3	cups all-purpose flour
4	teaspoons baking powder
1/2	teaspoon salt
1	cup milk
1-1/2	cups fresh *or* frozen blueberries

STREUSEL:

1/2	cup sugar
1/3	cup all-purpose flour
1/2	teaspoon ground cinnamon
1/4	cup cold butter

◆ In a large bowl, cream butter and sugar. Beat in egg and vanilla; mix well. Combine the flour, baking powder and salt; add to creamed mixture alternately with milk. Fold in blueberries.

◆ Fill 12 greased or paper-lined muffin cups two-thirds full. In a small bowl, combine the sugar, flour and cinnamon; cut in butter until crumbly. Sprinkle over muffins. Bake at 375° for 25-30 minutes or until browned. Cool for 5 minutes before removing to a wire rack. Serve warm.

YIELD: 12 SERVINGS.

Editor's Note: If using frozen blueberries, do not thaw before adding to batter.

CINNAMON DOUGHNUT MUFFINS

All five of our children are now grown with children of their own. Back when they were youngsters, however, they loved these treats as an after-school snack and as part of our Sunday brunch.

—Sharon Pullen, Alvinston, Ontario

1-3/4	cups all-purpose flour
1-1/2	teaspoons baking powder
1/2	teaspoon salt
1/2	teaspoon ground nutmeg
1/4	teaspoon ground cinnamon
3/4	cups sugar
1/3	cup canola oil
1	egg, lightly beaten
3/4	cup milk

Jam

TOPPING:

1/4	cup butter, melted
1/3	cup sugar
1	teaspoon ground cinnamon

◆ In a large bowl, combine flour, baking powder, salt, nutmeg and cinnamon. In a small bowl, combine sugar, oil, egg and milk; stir into dry ingredients just until moistened.

◆ Fill greased or paper-lined muffin cups half full; place 1 teaspoon jam on top. Cover jam with enough batter to fill muffin cups three-fourths full. Bake at 350° for 20-25 minutes or until a toothpick comes out clean.

◆ Place melted butter in a small bowl; combine sugar and cinnamon in another bowl. Immediately after removing muffins from the oven, dip tops in butter, then in cinnamon-sugar. Serve warm.

YIELD: 10 SERVINGS.

APPLE STREUSEL MUFFINS

I was looking for something warm to make for my daughter before school on a rainy morning. So I jazzed up a boxed muffin mix with a chopped apple, walnuts, brown sugar and a fast-to-fix vanilla glaze. The tasty results really hit the spot.

—*Elizabeth Calabrese, Yucaipa, California*

1	package (6-1/2 ounces) apple cinnamon muffin mix
1	large tart apple, peeled and diced
1/3	cup chopped walnuts
3	tablespoons brown sugar
4-1/2	teaspoons all-purpose flour
1	tablespoon butter, melted

GLAZE:

3/4	cup confectioners' sugar
1/2	teaspoon vanilla extract
1	to 2 tablespoons milk

◆ Prepare muffin mix according to package directions; fold in apple.

◆ Fill greased muffin cups three-fourths full. In a small bowl, combine the walnuts, brown sugar, flour and butter; sprinkle over batter.

◆ Bake at 400° for 15-20 minutes or until a toothpick comes out clean. Cool for 5 minutes before removing from pan to a wire rack. Combine the glaze ingredients; lightly drizzle over warm muffins.

YIELD: 6 SERVINGS.

LUSCIOUS LEMON MUFFINS

I've had this recipe since my college days, when it was served in one of my culinary art classes. These tempting, light and lemony muffins go well at a luncheon with chicken salad. Even our children love to munch on them.

—*Mary-Lynne Mason, Janesville, Wisconsin*

1/2	cup butter, softened
1/2	cup sugar
2	eggs, *separated*
1	cup all-purpose flour
1	teaspoon baking powder
1/4	teaspoon salt
3	tablespoons lemon juice
1	tablespoon grated lemon peel

Cinnamon-sugar

◆ In a bowl, cream butter and sugar. Add egg yolks; mix well. Combine flour, baking powder and salt; add alternately with lemon juice to creamed mixture. Beat egg whites until stiff peaks form; fold into batter with lemon peel.

◆ Fill greased or paper-lined muffin cups two-thirds full. Sprinkle with cinnamon-sugar. Bake at 350° for 20-25 minutes or until light golden brown and a toothpick inserted in the center comes out clean.

YIELD: 9 SERVINGS.

Breakfast Bliss

When you want fresh muffins in the morning, do some of the prep work the night before by combining the dry ingredients in a plastic bag and measuring any other ingredients that will hold. The following morning, quickly stir together the batter and pop the muffins in the oven. The aroma will lure everyone down to the kitchen in no time!

PEANUT BUTTER OAT MUFFINS

While teaching a home economics class, I asked students to personalize a basic muffin recipe. Two students created these peanut-packed snacks. The entire class agreed that the recipe was a winner.

—Elaine Searer, McVeytown, Pennsylvania

1-1/4	cups all-purpose flour
3/4	cup quick-cooking oats
3/4	cup packed brown sugar
3	teaspoons baking powder
1/2	teaspoon salt

Dash ground cinnamon

1	egg
1/4	cup peanut butter
1-1/4	cups milk
1/2	cup chopped peanuts

Whipped topping and additional peanuts, optional

◆ In a bowl, combine the flour, oats, brown sugar, baking powder, salt and cinnamon. In another bowl, beat the egg, peanut butter and milk until smooth. Stir into dry ingredients just until moistened. Fold in peanuts. Fill greased or paper-lined muffin cups three-fourths full. Bake at 375° for 15-18 minutes or until a toothpick comes out clean. Cool for 5 minutes before removing from pan to a wire rack. Serve with whipped topping and peanuts if desired.

YIELD: 12 SERVINGS.

Editor's Note: Reduced-fat or generic brands of peanut butter are not recommended for this recipe.

LEMON RASPBERRY JUMBO MUFFINS

These are my favorite muffins because they can be made with blueberries instead of raspberries with the same delicious results. Friends often request the recipe.

—Carol Thoreson, Rockford, Illinois

2	cups all-purpose flour
1	cup sugar
3	teaspoons baking powder
1/2	teaspoon salt
2	eggs
1	cup half-and-half cream
1/2	cup canola oil
1	teaspoon lemon extract
1	cup fresh *or* frozen unsweetened raspberries

◆ Fill greased jumbo muffin cups two-thirds full. Bake at 400° for 22-25 minutes or until a toothpick comes out clean. Cool for 5 minutes before removing from pan to a wire rack. Serve warm.

YIELD: 8 JUMBO-SIZE SERVINGS.

Editor's Note: If using frozen raspberries, do not thaw before adding to the batter. Sixteen regular-size muffin cups may be used; bake muffins for 18-20 minutes.

◆ In a large bowl, combine the flour, sugar, baking powder and salt. In another bowl, combine the eggs, cream, oil and extract. Stir into dry ingredients just until moistened. Fold in raspberries.

COFFEE CAKE MUFFINS

I combine the dry ingredients for these muffins the night before baking. In the morning, I add the remaining items, fill the muffin cups and pop them in the oven. Brown sugar, cinnamon and pecans give them a coffee cake-like flavor.

—Margaret McNeil, Memphis, Tennessee

1/4	cup packed brown sugar
1/4	cup chopped pecans
1	teaspoon ground cinnamon
1-1/2	cups all-purpose flour
1/2	cup sugar
2	teaspoons baking powder
1/4	teaspoon baking soda
1/4	teaspoon salt
1	egg
3/4	cup milk
1/3	cup canola oil

GLAZE:

1/2	cup confectioners' sugar
1	tablespoon milk
1	teaspoon vanilla extract

◆ In a small bowl, combine the brown sugar, pecans and cinnamon; set aside. In a large bowl, combine the flour, sugar, baking powder, baking soda and salt. In another bowl, beat the egg, milk and oil; stir into dry ingredients just until moistened.

◆ Spoon 1 tablespoon of batter into paper-lined muffin cups. Top each with 1 teaspoon nut mixture and about 2 tablespoons batter. Sprinkle with the remaining nut mixture. Bake at 400° for 22-24 minutes or until a toothpick comes out clean. Cool for 5 minutes before removing from pan to a wire rack.

◆ Combine glaze ingredients; spoon over muffins.

YIELD: 12 SERVINGS.

RASPBERRY CHOCOLATE CHIP MUFFINS

Yummy chocolate and luscious berries create bursts of sweetness in these treats. My family enjoys the muffins even before they are done baking because they make the kitchen smell so heavenly!

—*Carol Schwammel, Antioch, California*

1-2/3   **cups all-purpose flour**
3/4   **cup quick-cooking oats**
2/3   **cup sugar**
2   **teaspoons baking powder**
1   **teaspoon baking soda**
1/4   **teaspoon ground cinnamon**
1   **egg, lightly beaten**
3/4   **cup fat-free milk**
1/3   **cup canola oil**
2   **tablespoons orange juice**
1   **teaspoon vanilla extract**
3/4   **cup fresh *or* frozen unsweetened raspberries**
1/2   **cup miniature semisweet chocolate chips**

◆ In a large bowl, combine the first six ingredients. Combine the egg, milk, oil, orange juice and vanilla; stir into dry ingredients just until moistened. Fold in raspberries and miniature chocolate chips.

◆ Fill paper-lined muffin cups or cups coated with cooking spray two-thirds full. Bake at 375° for 20-25 minutes or until a toothpick comes out clean. Cool for 5 minutes before removing from pan to a wire rack.

YIELD: 12 SERVINGS.

Editor's Note: If using frozen raspberries, do not thaw before adding to batter.

POPPY SEED LEMONADE MUFFINS

It's hard to beat the delicious combination of flavors baked into these lemony muffins. The lightly glazed gems are so tasty that my gang looks forward to them for dessert.

—*Karen Ann Bland, Gove, Kansas*

    2   cups all-purpose flour
    9   tablespoons sugar, *divided*
    4   teaspoons poppy seeds
    3   teaspoons baking powder
  1/2   teaspoon salt
  3/4   cup lemonade concentrate, *divided*
  1/2   cup milk
  1/3   cup butter, melted
    1   egg

◆ In a large bowl, combine the flour, 5 tablespoons sugar, poppy seeds, baking powder and salt. In another bowl, combine 1/2 cup lemonade concentrate, milk, butter and egg until blended. Stir into dry ingredients just until combined.

◆ Fill greased or paper-lined muffin cups three-fourths full. Bake at 400° for 15-20 minutes or until a toothpick comes out clean. Cool for 5 minutes before removing from pan to a wire rack.

◆ In a small bowl, combine the remaining sugar and lemonade concentrate. Pierce muffin tops several items with a fork; drizzle with lemonade mixture.

YIELD: 12 SERVINGS.

S'MORE JUMBO MUFFINS

My daughter loves marshmallows, graham crackers and chocolate, so I came up with this muffin just for her. Each bite reminds us of camping out during the summer with good friends and making s'mores by the campfire.

—*Pam Ivbuls, Omaha, Nebraska*

  1-1/2   cups all-purpose flour
    1/2   cup graham cracker crumbs (about 8 squares)
    1/4   cup packed brown sugar
      1   teaspoon baking soda
    1/2   teaspoon salt
      1   egg
  1-1/2   cups buttermilk
    1/4   cup canola oil
    3/4   cup semisweet chocolate chips
  1-1/4   cups miniature marshmallows, *divided*

◆ In a large bowl, combine the dry ingredients. Combine the egg, buttermilk and oil; mix well. Stir egg mixture into dry ingredients just until moistened. Fold in chocolate chips and 1 cup marshmallows.

◆ Fill greased jumbo muffin cups three-fourths full. Sprinkle with remaining marshmallows. Bake at 375° for 18-20 minutes or until a toothpick comes out clean. Cool for 5 minutes before removing from pan to a wire rack. Serve warm.

YIELD: 6 SERVINGS.

PAT'S BLUEBERRY MUFFINS

Yummy and golden, these muffins are packed with plenty of berries and are a great addition to a breakfast or brunch menu. But at our house, muffins aren't relegated to mornings—we also enjoy them with supper or for anytime snacks.

—Patricia Throlson, Willmar, Minnesota

2	cups all-purpose flour
1/3	cup plus 2 tablespoons sugar
1	tablespoon baking powder
1	teaspoon salt
1	cup fresh *or* frozen blueberries, thawed
1	egg
1	cup milk
1/4	cup butter, melted

◆ In a large bowl, combine flour, sugar, baking powder and salt. Add the blueberries. In another bowl, beat egg and milk; stir in butter. Stir into dry ingredients just until moistened.

◆ Fill greased or paper-lined muffin cups two-thirds full. Bake at 400° for 20-25 minutes or until the muffins test done.

YIELD: 12 SERVINGS.

TROPICAL MUFFINS

I entered these muffins at our county fair and won the grand champion award for baked goods. They're so moist and tender, you won't need to add extra butter.

—Sylvia Osborn, Clay Center, Kansas

1/4	cup butter, softened
1/2	cup sugar
1	egg
1	cup (8 ounces) sour cream
1-1/2	teaspoons rum extract
1-1/2	cups all-purpose flour
1	teaspoon baking powder
1/2	teaspoon baking soda
1/2	teaspoon salt
1	can (8 ounces) crushed pineapple, drained
1/2	cup flaked coconut
1/3	cup chopped pecans

◆ In a large bowl, cream the butter and sugar until light and fluffy. Beat in the egg, sour cream and extract. Combine the flour, baking powder, baking soda and salt; stir into the creamed mixture just until moistened. Fold in the pineapple, coconut and pecans.

◆ Fill greased or paper-lined muffin cups two-thirds full. Bake at 375° for 22-25 minutes or until a toothpick comes out clean. Cool for 5 minutes before removing from pan to a wire rack.

YIELD: 12 SERVINGS.

MAPLE-DRIZZLED APPLE MUFFINS

I've been baking for years and enjoy seeing the smiles on family members' faces whenever they sample one of my treats...like these delicious muffins.

—*Sarah Brodersen, Herman, Nebraska*

1-1/3	cups all-purpose flour
1	cup quick-cooking oats
2/3	cup sugar
1	tablespoon baking powder
1-1/2	teaspoons ground cinnamon
1/2	cup milk
1/3	cup butter, melted
1/4	cup maple syrup
1	egg, lightly beaten
2	cups chopped peeled apples
12	pecan halves

GLAZE:

1/3	cup confectioners' sugar
2	tablespoons maple syrup

◆ In a large bowl, combine the flour, oats, sugar, baking powder and cinnamon. In a small bowl, mix milk, butter, syrup and egg; stir into dry ingredients just until moistened. Fold in apples.

◆ Fill greased or paper-lined muffin cups three-fourths full. Top each with a pecan half. Bake at 400° for 18-20 minutes or until a toothpick comes out clean. Cool for 10 minutes before removing from pan to a wire rack to cool completely.

◆ For glaze, mix confectioners' sugar and syrup; drizzle over muffins.

YIELD: 12 SERVINGS.

CREAM CHEESE APPLE MUFFINS

My husband likes to take these rich, moist muffins to work, then warm them up in the microwave for his morning snack. Our three daughters love them, too. My home smells wonderful while they're baking.

—Marcia Hill, Byron Center, Michigan

1	package (3 ounces) cream cheese, softened
3/4	cup sugar
2	eggs
1/2	cup milk
1/4	cup butter, melted
1	tablespoon lemon juice
1	teaspoon vanilla extract
1-1/2	cups all-purpose flour
1-1/2	teaspoons baking powder
1/2	teaspoon baking soda
1/2	teaspoon salt
1	cup diced peeled tart apples
1/2	cup bran flakes

TOPPING:

1-1/2	teaspoons sugar
1	teaspoon ground cinnamon

◆ In a bowl, combine the cream cheese, sugar, eggs, milk, butter, lemon juice and vanilla; beat until smooth. Combine the flour, baking powder, baking soda and salt; stir into cream cheese mixture just until moistened. Fold in the apples and bran flakes.

◆ Fill greased or paper-lined muffin cups two-thirds full. Combine topping ingredients; sprinkle over batter. Bake at 375° for 20-25 minutes or until a toothpick comes out clean. Cool for 5 minutes before removing from pan to a wire rack.

YIELD: 12 SERVINGS.

TOUCH OF SPRING MUFFINS

Strawberries and rhubarb are a winning combination, and their sweet-tart pairing makes these lovely muffins delightful as part of a meal or as a snack. Remember this recipe when your backyard rhubarb is ready to cut or you see fresh stalks at the store.

—Gail Sykora, Menomonee Falls, Wisconsin

2	cups all-purpose flour
1/2	cup sugar
1	tablespoon baking powder
1/2	teaspoon salt
1	egg
3/4	cup milk
1/3	cup canola oil
1/2	cup sliced fresh strawberries
1/2	cup sliced fresh rhubarb

TOPPING:

6	small fresh strawberries, halved
2	teaspoons sugar

◆ In a large bowl, combine flour, sugar, baking powder and salt. In another bowl, beat egg, milk and oil until smooth. Stir into dry ingredients just until moistened. Fold in strawberries and rhubarb.

◆ Fill greased or paper-lined muffin cups three-fourths full. Place a strawberry half, cut side down, on each. Sprinkle with sugar. Bake at 375° for 22-25 minutes or until muffins test done. Cool muffins for 5 minutes before removing from pan to a wire rack. Serve warm.

YIELD: 12 SERVINGS.

BANANA CHIP MUFFINS

I combined a few recipes to come up with these banana muffins. The chocolate chips often surprise people who try them. Our four boys make these disappear in a hurry, so I usually double the recipe.

—Colleen Johnson, Elbridge, New York

1-3/4	cups all-purpose flour
1/4	cup sugar
2-1/2	teaspoons baking powder
3/4	teaspoon salt
1	egg
1/2	cup milk
1/3	cup canola oil
1/2	cup mashed ripe banana
1/2	cup unsweetened applesauce
1	cup miniature semisweet chocolate chips

◆ In a large bowl, combine the flour, sugar, baking powder and salt. In another bowl, combine the egg, milk, oil, banana and applesauce; stir into dry ingredients just until moistened. Fold in the chocolate chips.

◆ Fill greased muffin cups two-thirds full. Bake at 400° for 20 minutes or until a toothpick comes out clean. Cool for 5 minutes before removing from pan to a wire rack.

YIELD: 12 SERVINGS.

CHOCOLATE MUFFINS

I first made these fancy nut-topped muffins for a Valentine's Day breakfast for my husband and son. Applesauce keeps them moist and eliminates the need for oil.

—Carol Gaus, Itasca, Illinois

1-1/4 cups all-purpose flour
1/2 cup sugar
1/3 cup baking cocoa
1 teaspoon baking powder
1 teaspoon baking soda
1 cup unsweetened applesauce
1/2 cup fat-free milk
1/2 cup egg substitute
1 teaspoon vanilla extract
1/4 cup sliced almonds

◆ In a bowl, combine the flour, sugar, cocoa, baking powder and baking soda. In another bowl, whisk the applesauce, milk, egg substitute and vanilla until smooth. Stir into dry ingredients just until moistened.

◆ Coat muffin cups with cooking spray; fill three-fourths full with batter. Sprinkle with almonds. Bake at 400° for 20-25 minutes or until muffins test done. Cool for 10 minutes; remove from pan to a wire rack.

YIELD: 12 SERVINGS.

COCONUT MUFFINS

I dressed up this muffin recipe with flaked coconut, coconut extract and a streusel topping to create these tender treats. We like them so much, they're a regular at Saturday morning breakfast.

—Sue Gronholz, Beaver Dam, Wisconsin

2 cups all-purpose flour
1/2 cup sugar
3 teaspoons baking powder
1/2 teaspoon salt
2/3 cup milk
1 egg
1/3 cup canola oil
1/2 teaspoon coconut extract
1/4 cup flaked coconut

TOPPING:
1/4 cup sugar
1/4 cup flaked coconut
1 tablespoon butter, softened
1/2 teaspoon ground cinnamon

◆ In a large bowl, combine the flour, sugar, baking powder and salt. In another bowl, combine the milk, egg, oil and extract. Stir into dry ingredients just until combined. Fold in coconut. Fill greased or paper-lined muffin cups two-thirds full.

◆ Combine the topping ingredients; sprinkle over batter. Bake at 400° for 18-20 minutes or until a toothpick comes out clean. Cool for 5 minutes before removing from pan to a wire rack. Serve warm.

YIELD: 8 SERVINGS.

PEACHES & CREAM MUFFINS

Breakfast muffins are a must at our house, and my family loves these not-too-sweet treats. Peaches star in these pretty crumb-topped muffins.

—*Deanne Bagley, Bath, New York*

1	egg
1/2	cup milk *or* sour cream
1/4	cup canola oil
1-1/2	cups all-purpose flour
1/2	cup sugar
2	teaspoons baking powder
1/2	teaspoon salt
1	cup chopped fresh *or* frozen peaches, thawed

◆ In a bowl, beat egg; add milk and oil. Combine flour, sugar, baking powder and salt; stir into the egg mixture just until moistened. Stir in the peaches.

◆ Fill greased or paper-lined muffin cups three-fourths full. Bake at 400° for 20-25 minutes or until a toothpick inserted in a muffin comes out clean. Cool for 5 minutes before removing from pan to a wire rack.

YIELD: 10 SERVINGS.

CRAN-APPLE MUFFINS

I like to pile these muffins on a plate when friends drop in for coffee. Even my grandkids enjoy the satisfying flavor combination of cranberry and apples.

—Millie Westland, Hayward, Minnesota

1/2	cup whole-berry cranberry sauce
1/2	teaspoon grated orange peel
1-1/2	cups all-purpose flour
1/2	cup sugar
1	teaspoon ground cinnamon
1/2	teaspoon baking soda
1/4	teaspoon baking powder
1/4	teaspoon salt
1	egg
1/3	cup milk
1/3	cup canola oil
1	cup shredded peeled tart apple
1/2	cup confectioners' sugar
1	tablespoon orange juice

◆ In a small bowl, combine cranberry sauce and orange peel; set aside. In a large bowl, combine the flour, sugar, cinnamon, baking soda, baking powder and salt. Beat the egg, milk and oil; stir into dry ingredients just until moistened. Fold in apple.

◆ Fill greased or paper-lined muffin cups half full. Make a well in the center of each muffin; fill with about 2 teaspoons of reserved cranberry mixture. Bake at 375° for 18-20 minutes or until a toothpick inserted in muffin comes out clean. Cool for 5 minutes before removing from pan to a wire rack. Combine confectioners' sugar and orange juice; drizzle over cooled muffins.

YIELD: 12 SERVINGS.

ORANGE BLOSSOM MUFFINS

My husband and I tasted a muffin similar to these at a bed-and-breakfast. When I told a friend about them, she shared her recipe for these moist and tender muffins. They are fun to serve full-size or as mini muffins at ladies' luncheons, tea parties or showers.

—*Rhonda Lyons, Marshall, Texas*

- 2 tablespoons plus 1/4 cup sugar, *divided*
- 4-1/2 teaspoons all-purpose flour
- 1/2 teaspoon ground cinnamon
- 1/4 teaspoon ground nutmeg
- 1 tablespoon cold butter
- 2 cups reduced-fat biscuit/baking mix
- 1 egg
- 1/2 cup orange juice
- 1/2 cup orange marmalade
- 2 tablespoons canola oil
- 1/4 cup chopped pecans

◆ In a small bowl, combine 2 tablespoons sugar, flour, cinnamon and nutmeg; cut in butter until crumbly. Set aside for topping. Place the biscuit mix in a bowl. Combine the egg, orange juice, marmalade, canola oil and remaining sugar; stir into biscuit mix just until moistened. Fold in pecans.

◆ Coat muffin cups with cooking spray or use paper liners; fill two-thirds full with batter. Sprinkle with reserved crumb mixture. Bake at 400° for 18-20 minutes or until a toothpick comes out clean. Cool for 5 minutes before removing from pan to a wire rack. Serve warm.

YIELD: 12 SERVINGS.

SUNSHINE MUFFINS

I use two convenient mixes to create these sweet corn bread muffins. The yellow cake mix gives them a smoother texture than traditional corn bread.

—*Linnea Rein, Topeka, Kansas*

- 2 eggs
- 1/2 cup water
- 1/3 cup milk
- 2 tablespoons canola oil
- 1 package (9 ounces) yellow cake mix
- 1 package (8-1/2 ounces) corn bread/muffin mix

◆ In a bowl, combine the eggs, water, milk and oil. Stir in mixes and mix well. Fill greased and floured muffin cups half full.

◆ Bake at 350° for 18-22 minutes or until a toothpick comes out clean. Cool for 5 minutes; remove from pans to wire racks.

YIELD: 14 SERVINGS.

Blue-Ribbon Specialties

WHETHER YOU'RE simply crazy for cupcakes or the neighborhood's famous muffin lady, you're likely to be on the prowl for the next great recipe. Look no further because you'll find a bonanza of prize-winning favorites in the selection of goodies offered here.

MINT BROWNIE CUPCAKES, P. 69

CHOCOLATE ORANGE CUPCAKES

Chocolate and orange are perfect together in these fudgy morsels. I add mayonnaise to give them a moist brownie-like texture. The cupcakes taste even better when served with a scoop of homemade ice cream.

—Shirley Brazel, Coos Bay, Oregon

1-1/2 cups all-purpose flour
1/2 cup sugar
1/4 cup baking cocoa
1 teaspoon baking soda
1/4 teaspoon salt
1/2 cup mayonnaise
1 teaspoon grated orange peel
1 teaspoon vanilla extract
1/2 cup orange juice
1/2 cup semisweet chocolate chips
Confectioners' sugar

◆ In a bowl, combine the flour, sugar, cocoa, baking soda and salt. In another bowl, combine the mayonnaise, orange peel and vanilla; gradually add orange juice until blended. Stir into dry ingredients just until combined. Stir in the chocolate chips (batter will be thick).

◆ Fill paper-lined muffin cups two-thirds full. Bake at 350° for 18-23 minutes or until a toothpick inserted in the center comes out clean. Cool for 10 minutes before removing from pan to a wire rack to cool completely. Dust with confectioners' sugar.

YIELD: 9 SERVINGS.

Editor's Note: Reduced-fat or fat-free mayonnaise is not recommended for use in this recipe.

CARAMEL APPLE CUPCAKES

Bring these extra-special cupcakes to your next potluck or bake sale and watch how quickly they disappear—if your family doesn't gobble them up first! Kids will go for the fun appearance and tasty toppings while adults will appreciate the tender spiced cake that sits underneath.

—Diane Halferty, Corpus Christi, Texas

1 package (18-1/4 ounces) spice cake mix *or* 1 pacakge (18 ounces) carrot cake mix
2 cups chopped peeled tart apples
20 caramels
3 tablespoons milk
1 cup finely chopped pecans, toasted
12 Popsicle sticks

◆ Prepare cake batter according to package directions; fold in apples.

◆ Fill 12 greased or paper-lined jumbo muffin cups three-fourths full. Bake at 350° for 20 minutes or until a toothpick comes out clean. Cool for 10 minutes before removing from pans to wire racks to cool completely.

◆ In a saucepan, cook the caramels and milk over low heat until smooth. Spread over cupcakes. Sprinkle with pecans. Insert a wooden stick into the center of each cupcake.

YIELD: 12 SERVINGS.

BURST O' LEMON MUFFINS

While I visited my sister in Florida, she baked a batch of these incredible muffins. They have a cake-like texture with sweet coconut and a mouth-watering lemon zing. I refused to go home without the recipe.

—Nancy Rader, Columbus, Ohio

1-3/4 cups all-purpose flour

3/4 cup sugar

1 teaspoon baking powder

3/4 teaspoon baking soda

1/4 teaspoon salt

1 cup (8 ounces) lemon *or* vanilla yogurt

1 egg

1/3 cup butter, melted

1 to 2 tablespoons grated lemon peel

1 tablespoon lemon juice

1/2 cup flaked coconut

TOPPING:

1/3 cup lemon juice

1/4 cup sugar

1/4 cup flaked coconut, toasted

◆ In a large bowl, combine the flour, sugar, baking powder, baking soda and salt. In a small bowl, beat the yogurt, egg, butter, lemon peel and lemon juice until smooth; stir into dry ingredients just until moistened. Fold in the coconut.

◆ Fill greased muffin cups two-thirds full. Bake at 400° for 18-22 minutes or until golden brown and toothpick inserted near the center comes out clean. Cool for 5 minutes before removing from pan to a wire rack.

◆ In a saucepan, combine the lemon juice and sugar; cook and stir over medium heat until sugar is dissolved. Stir in coconut. Using a toothpick, poke 6-8 holes in each muffin. Spoon the coconut mixture over muffins. Serve the muffins warm or cool to room temperature.

YIELD: 12 SERVINGS.

CHOCOLATE BANANA SPLIT CUPCAKES

My mom often made these cute cupcakes when I was young to satisfy my sweet tooth. They go over just as well now when I bake them for my own children.

—Lorelie Miller, Benito, Manitoba

1-1/4	cups all-purpose flour
1/2	cup sugar
1/4	teaspoon baking soda
1/4	teaspoon salt
1/2	cup mashed banana (about 1 medium)
1/2	cup butter, melted
1/4	cup buttermilk
1	egg, lightly beaten
1/2	teaspoon vanilla extract
1/2	cup chopped walnuts
2	milk chocolate bars (1.55 ounces *each*) broken into squares, *divided*

FROSTING:

1-1/2	cups confectioners' sugar
1	tablespoon butter, melted
1/2	teaspoon vanilla extract
1	to 2 tablespoons milk
12	maraschino cherries with stems

◆ In a bowl, combine the flour, sugar, baking soda and salt. In another bowl, combine the banana, butter, buttermilk, egg and vanilla. Add to the dry ingredients; stir just until combined. Fold in the nuts. Spoon 1 tablespoon of batter into each paper-lined muffin cup. Top each with one candy bar square. Fill the remainder of the cup two-thirds full with batter.

◆ Bake at 350° for 20-25 minutes or until a toothpick inserted in the cupcake comes out clean. Cool for 10 minutes before removing from pan to a wire rack to cool completely.

◆ In a bowl, combine the confectioners' sugar, butter, vanilla and enough milk to achieve spreading consistency. Frost cooled cupcakes. In a microwave, melt remaining candy bar squares; drizzle over frosting. Top each with a cherry.

YIELD: 12 SERVINGS.

SPICED PEAR MUFFINS

I received this outstanding recipe from the custodian at our church, who whips up these moist, fruity muffins and shares them with friends. He gave me one to try a few years ago, and I was hooked. The tasty combination of pears and spices is irresistible.

—*Linda Jachimstal, Manitowoc, Wisconsin*

2 cups all-purpose flour
1/2 cup packed brown sugar
2 teaspoons ground ginger
1 teaspoon baking soda
1 teaspoon ground cinnamon
1/2 teaspoon salt
1/8 teaspoon ground nutmeg
1/8 teaspoon ground cloves
1 egg
1 cup (8 ounces) plain yogurt
1/2 cup canola oil
3 tablespoons molasses
1-1/2 cups finely chopped peeled pears (about 2 medium)
1/2 cup raisins
1/3 cup chopped walnuts

◆ In a large bowl, combine the first eight ingredients. In another bowl, beat the egg, yogurt, oil and molasses until smooth. Stir into dry ingredients just until moistened. Fold in pears, raisins and walnuts.

◆ Fill greased or paper-lined miniature muffin cups two-thirds full. Bake at 400° for 10-12 minutes or until muffins test done. Cool for 5 minutes before removing from pans to wire racks. Serve warm.

YIELD: 24 MINI SERVINGS OR 16 REGULAR SERVINGS.

TRIPLE BERRY MUFFINS

Fresh blueberries, raspberries and strawberries bring eye-catching color to these tender muffins nicely spiced with ground cinnamon. They come together in no time and bake up in a snap.

—*Michelle Turnis, Hopkinton, Iowa*

3 cups all-purpose flour
1-1/2 cups sugar
4-1/2 teaspoons ground cinnamon
3 teaspoons baking powder
1/2 teaspoon salt
1/2 teaspoon baking soda
2 eggs
1-1/4 cups milk
1 cup butter, melted
1 cup fresh blueberries
1/2 cup fresh raspberries
1/2 cup chopped fresh strawberries

◆ In a large bowl, combine the first six ingredients. In another bowl, beat the eggs, milk and butter; stir into dry ingredients just until moistened. Fold in the berries.

◆ Fill greased or paper-lined muffin cups three-fourths full. Bake at 375° for 18-20 minutes or until a toothpick comes out clean. Cool for 5 minutes before removing from pans to wire racks.

YIELD: 18 SERVINGS.

BERRY PLEASING MUFFINS

These are scrumptious with sausage and scrambled eggs for breakfast or with cottage cheese and a sliced apple for a light lunch. The handheld snacks also make a coffee break special and afternoon tea a real treat.

—Julie Wood, Vancouver, Washington

1	cup fresh *or* frozen blueberries
1/2	cup chopped fresh *or* frozen cranberries
1	cup sugar, *divided*
1	package (8 ounces) cream cheese, softened
2	eggs
1	teaspoon vanilla extract
1	cup all-purpose flour
1	teaspoon baking soda
1/2	teaspoon salt
1/4	teaspoon ground nutmeg

TOPPING:

1/4	cup finely chopped walnuts
1/4	cup flaked coconut
2	tablespoons brown sugar
1/4	teaspoon ground cinnamon

◆ In a large bowl, combine blueberries, cranberries and 1/4 cup sugar; set aside. In another large bowl, beat cream cheese and remaining sugar until smooth. Add eggs, one at a time, beating well after each addition. Beat in vanilla. In a bowl, combine the flour, baking soda, salt and nutmeg; add to the creamed mixture. Fold in the berry mixture.

◆ Fill greased or paper-lined muffin cups two-thirds full. Combine topping ingredients; sprinkle over batter. Bake at 400° for 18-20 minutes or until a toothpick comes out clean. Cool muffins for 5 minutes before removing to a wire rack.

YIELD: 12 SERVINGS.

CRANBERRY CREAM CHEESE MUFFINS

The sweet, creamy filling in these cranberry muffins makes them popular at my house. The tender treats also have a crispy sugar topping that is bound to be a hit.

—Sharon Hartman, Twin Falls, Idaho

1	package (3 ounces) cream cheese, softened
4	tablespoons sugar, *divided*
1	package (15.6 ounces) cranberry-orange quick bread mix
1	cup milk
1/3	cup canola oil
1	egg

◆ In a small bowl, beat the cream cheese and 2 tablespoons sugar until smooth; set aside. Place bread mix in another bowl. Combine the milk, oil and egg; stir into bread mix just until moistened.

◆ Fill paper-lined muffin cups one-fourth full with batter. Place 2 teaspoons cream cheese mixture in the center of each; top with remaining batter. Sprinkle with remaining sugar. Bake at 400° for 18-20 minutes or until a toothpick comes out clean. Cool for 5 minutes before removing from pan to a wire rack.

YIELD: 12 SERVINGS.

MINT BROWNIE CUPCAKES

These minty treats are so rich and chocolately, it begs the question…are they a cupcake or a brownie? Either way, they're a favorite at parties and potlucks and are always gobbled up fast!

—*Carol Maertz, Spruce Grove, Alberta*

  1   **cup mint chocolate chips**
 1/2 **cup butter, cubed**
 1/2 **cup sugar**
  2   **eggs**
 1/2 **cup all-purpose flour**
  1   **teaspoon baking powder**
TOPPING:
  4   **cups miniature marshmallows**
 3/4 **cup milk**
 1-1/2 **teaspoons peppermint extract**
Green *or* red food coloring, optional
 1-1/2 **cups heavy whipping cream, whipped**
Additional chocolate chips, optional

◆ In a heavy saucepan, melt chips and butter; stir until smooth. Remove from the heat.

◆ Stir in sugar and eggs. Combine flour and baking powder; gradually stir into chocolate mixture until smooth.

◆ Fill paper-lined muffin cups half full. Bake at 350° for 15-20 minutes or until a toothpick inserted in the center comes out clean (cupcakes may fall in center). Remove from pan to a wire rack to cool.

◆ In a large saucepan, cook and stir marshmallows and milk over low heat until smooth. Remove from the heat; stir in extract and food coloring, if desired.

◆ Cover and refrigerate for about 15 minutes or until cooled. Fold in whipped cream. Spread over cupcakes or top each with a dollop of topping. Refrigerate for at least 1 hour. Sprinkle with additional chocolate chips if desired. Store in the refrigerator.

YIELD: 16 SERVINGS.

Editor's Note: If mint chocolate chips are not available, place 2 cups (12 ounces) semisweet chocolate chips and 1/4 teaspoon peppermint extract in a plastic bag; seal and toss to coat. Allow chips to stand for 24-48 hours.

COCONUT CUPCAKES

I took these yummy treats to a picnic for our computer club one year, and they went like hotcakes! With their creamy frosting and sprinkling of coconut, they appeal to kids and adults alike.

—*Judy Wilson, Sun City West, Arizona*

1-1/2   cups butter, softened
2   cups sugar
5   eggs
1   to 1-1/2 teaspoons vanilla extract
1   to 1-1/2 teaspoons almond extract
3   cups all-purpose flour
1   teaspoon baking powder
1/2   teaspoon baking soda
1/2   teaspoon salt
1   cup buttermilk
1-1/4   cups flaked coconut

CREAM CHEESE FROSTING:

1   package (8 ounces) cream cheese, softened
3/4   cup butter, softened
1/2   teaspoon vanilla extract
1/2   teaspoon almond extract
2-3/4   cups confectioners' sugar
Additional flaked coconut, toasted

◆ In a large bowl, cream butter and sugar until light and fluffy. Add eggs, one at a time, beating well after each addition. Beat in extracts. Combine the flour, baking powder, baking soda and salt; add to creamed mixture alternately with buttermilk, beating well after each addition. Fold in coconut.

◆ Fill paper-lined muffin cups two-thirds full. Bake at 350° for 18-20 minutes or until a toothpick comes out clean. Cool for 10 minutes before removing from pans to wire racks to cool completely.

◆ For frosting, in a large bowl, beat the cream cheese, butter and extracts until smooth. Gradually beat in confectioners' sugar. Frost cupcakes; sprinkle with toasted coconut.

YIELD: 30 SERVINGS.

TANGERINE MUFFINS

I love preparing baked goods and sharing them with family and friends. These light yet flavorful muffins are always such a hit that I often end up sharing the recipe as well.
—Margaret Yerkes, New Port Richey, Florida

2	cups all-purpose flour
1/2	cup sugar
2	teaspoons baking powder
1	teaspoon baking soda
1/2	teaspoon salt
1	carton (8 ounces) vanilla yogurt
1	egg, lightly beaten
1/4	cup butter, melted
2	tablespoons milk
1	cup diced peeled tangerine
1	tablespoon grated tangerine peel

◆ In a bowl, combine the first five ingredients. In a small bowl, combine the yogurt, egg, butter and milk until smooth; stir into dry ingredients just until moistened. Stir in tangerine and grated peel.

◆ Fill greased or paper-lined muffin cups two-thirds full. Bake at 400° for 18-20 minutes or until a toothpick comes out clean. Cool for 5 minutes before removing from pan to wire rack.

YIELD: 12 SERVINGS.

PEANUT BUTTER & JELLY MINI MUFFINS

Everyone will fall in love with these mini jelly-filled treats. Packed with peanut butter flavor, they're a fun and easy way to start off the day or to share as an after-school snack.
—Vickie Barrow, Edenton, North Carolina

1	cup all-purpose flour
1/3	cup packed brown sugar
1	teaspoon baking powder
1/2	teaspoon baking soda
1/4	teaspoon salt
2	eggs
1/2	cup vanilla yogurt
3	tablespoons creamy peanut butter
2	tablespoons canola oil
3	tablespoons strawberry *or* grape jelly

◆ In a large bowl, combine the flour, brown sugar, baking powder, baking soda and salt. In a small bowl, beat the eggs, yogurt, peanut butter and oil on low speed until smooth; stir mixture into the dry ingredients just until moistened.

◆ Fill greased or paper-lined miniature muffin cups half full. Top each with 1/4 teaspoon jelly and remaining batter. Bake at 400° for 10-12 minutes or until golden brown. Cool for 5 minutes before removing from pans to wire racks.

YIELD: 30 SERVINGS.

SHOOFLY CUPCAKES

These moist, old-fashioned molasses cupcakes were my grandmother's specialty. To keep them from disappearing too quickly, she used to store them out of sight. Somehow, we always found her hiding places!

—Beth Adams, Jacksonville, Florida

4 cups all-purpose flour
2 cups packed brown sugar
1/4 teaspoon salt
1 cup cold butter, cubed
2 teaspoons baking soda
2 cups boiling water
1 cup molasses

◆ In a large bowl, combine the flour, brown sugar and salt. Cut in butter until crumbly. Set aside 1 cup of crumb mixture for topping. Add baking soda to remaining mixture. Stir in the water and molasses.

◆ Fill paper-lined muffin cups two-thirds full. Sprinkle with reserved crumb mixture. Bake at 350° for 20-25 minutes or until a toothpick inserted near the center comes out clean. Cool for 10 minutes before removing from pans to wire racks to cool.

YIELD: 24 SERVINGS.

Editor's Note: This recipe does not use eggs.

CREAM CHEESE CHOCOLATE CUPCAKES

Smooth cream cheese inside these cupcakes makes them so rich. The classic combination of peanut butter and chocolate chips comes through in every yummy bite. You'll be asked to make them again and again.

—Shirley Dunbar, Mojave, California

1 package (8 ounces) cream cheese, softened
1/3 cup sugar
1 egg
1/8 teaspoon salt
1 cup semisweet chocolate chips
1 cup peanut butter chips

CUPCAKES:
1 cup sugar
1 cup water
1/3 cup canola oil
1 tablespoon white vinegar
1 teaspoon vanilla extract
1-1/2 cups all-purpose flour
1/4 cup baking cocoa
1 teaspoon baking soda
1/2 teaspoon salt

◆ In a large bowl, beat cream cheese until fluffy. Beat the sugar, egg and salt smooth. Fold in chocolate and peanut butter chips; set aside.

◆ For cupcakes, in a large bowl, beat the sugar, water, oil, vinegar and vanilla until well blended. In a large bowl, combine the flour, cocoa, baking soda and salt; gradually beat into sugar mixture until blended.

◆ Fill paper-lined muffin cups half full with batter. Top each with about 2 tablespoons of the cream cheese mixture. Bake at 350° for 25-30 minutes or until toothpick inserted into cupcake comes out clean. Cool for 10 minutes before removing from pans to wire racks to cool completely.

YIELD: 18 SERVINGS.

CHOCOLATE COOKIE MUFFINS

I'm always on the lookout for new ways to make muffins. This fun version includes crushed, cream-filled chocolate cookies in the batter. They're a double treat—it's like a muffin and a cookie in one!

—Jan Blue, Cuyahoga Falls, Ohio

1-3/4   **cups all-purpose flour**
1/4   **cup sugar**
3   **teaspoons baking powder**
1/3   **cup cold butter**
1   **egg**
1   **cup milk**
16   **cream-filled chocolate sandwich cookies, coarsely chopped**

TOPPING:

3   **tablespoons all-purpose flour**
3   **tablespoons sugar**
5   **cream-filled chocolate sandwich cookies, finely crushed**
2   **tablespoons cold butter**
1   **cup vanilla *or* white chips**
1   **tablespoon shortening**

◆ In a large bowl, combine the flour, sugar and baking powder. Cut in butter until mixture resembles coarse crumbs. Beat egg and milk; stir into dry ingredients just until moistened. Fold in chopped cookies. Fill greased muffin cups two-thirds full.

◆ For topping, combine the flour, sugar and crushed cookies. Cut in the butter until crumbly; sprinkle about 1 tablespoon over each muffin. Bake at 400° for 16-18 minutes or until a toothpick comes out clean. Cool for 5 minutes before removing from pan to a wire rack.

◆ In a heavy saucepan over low heat, melt vanilla chips and shortening until smooth. Lightly drizzle over cooled muffins.

YIELD: 12 SERVINGS.

CARROT CUPCAKES

To get my family to eat more vegetables, I often "hide" nutritious ingredients inside sweet treats. The carrots add wonderful moistness to these cupcakes, which have a rich cream cheese frosting. Now we can have our cake and eat our vegetables, too!

—Doreen Kelly, Rosyln, Pennsylvania

4	eggs
2	cups sugar
1	cup canola oil
2	cups all-purpose flour
2	teaspoons ground cinnamon
1	teaspoon baking soda
1	teaspoon baking powder
1	teaspoon ground allspice
1/2	teaspoon salt
3	cups grated carrots

CHUNKY FROSTING:

1	package (8 ounces) cream cheese, softened
1/4	cup butter, softened
2	cups confectioners' sugar
1/2	cup flaked coconut
1/2	cup chopped pecans
1/2	cup chopped raisins

◆ In a large bowl, beat the eggs, sugar and oil. Combine the flour, cinnamon, baking soda, baking powder, allspice and salt; gradually add to egg mixture. Stir in carrots.

◆ Fill greased or paper-lined muffin cups two-thirds full. Bake at 325° for 20-25 minutes or until a toothpick comes out clean. Cool cupcakes for 5 minutes before removing from pans to wire racks.

◆ For frosting, in a large bowl, beat cream cheese and butter until fluffy. Gradually beat in confectioners' sugar until smooth. Stir in the coconut, pecans and raisins. Frost cupcakes. Store in the refrigerator.

YIELD: 24 SERVINGS.

LEMON SPARKLE CUPCAKES

Bursting with lemony zing, these cupcakes don't require frosting. In fact, my family prefers the crunchy sugar-and-spice topping. A dear friend shared the recipe with me, and it has long been in demand at our house.

—Janice Porter, Platte, South Dakota

2/3	cup shortening
1	cup sugar
3	eggs
1-2/3	cups all-purpose flour
2-1/2	teaspoons baking powder
1/2	teaspoon salt
2/3	cup milk
1	tablespoon grated lemon peel

TOPPING:

1/4	cup sugar
1	tablespoon grated lemon peel
1/8	teaspoon ground nutmeg

◆ In a large bowl, cream shortening and sugar until light and fluffy. Add eggs, one at a time, beating well after each addition. Combine the flour, baking powder and salt; add to the creamed mixture alternately with milk, beating well after each addition. Stir in the lemon peel.

◆ Fill paper-lined muffin cups two-thirds full. Combine the topping ingredients; sprinkle a rounded 1/2 teaspoonful over each cupcake. Bake at 350° for 20-24 minutes or until a toothpick comes out clean. Cool for 10 minutes before removing from pans to wire racks to cool completely.

YIELD: 15 SERVINGS.

CHOCOLATE-COCONUT ANGEL CUPCAKES

These cupcakes don't taste light at all. In fact, my guests always come back for a second treat. The meringue-like tops make them different, but it is the chocolate and coconut that make them memorable.

—Bernice Janowski, Stevens Point, Wisconsin

6	egg whites
1-1/3	cups sugar, *divided*
2/3	cup all-purpose flour
1/4	cup baking cocoa
1/2	teaspoon baking powder
1	teaspoon almond extract
1/2	teaspoon cream of tartar
1/4	teaspoon salt
1	cup flaked coconut

◆ Place egg whites in a large bowl; let stand at room temperature for 30 minutes. Combine 1 cup sugar, flour, cocoa and baking powder. Sift together twice; set aside.

◆ Add the almond extract, cream of tartar and salt to egg whites; beat on medium speed until soft peaks form. Gradually add the remaining sugar, about 2 tablespoons at a time, beating on high until stiff, glossy peaks form. Gradually fold in the cocoa mixture, about 1/2 cup at a time. Gently fold in coconut.

◆ Fill paper-lined muffin cups two-thirds full. Bake at 350° for 30-35 minutes or until golden brown and top appears dry. Cool for 10 minutes before removing from pans to wire racks.

YIELD: 18 SERVINGS.

Egg-cellent Idea

Don't fret if a recipe calls for egg whites or egg yolk. Separating them is easy with the help of an egg separator. Simply place the egg separator over a custard cup; crack the egg into the separator. As each egg is separated, place the yolk in one custard cup and empty the egg whites into another. It's easiest to separate eggs when they are cold.

BROWNIE KISS CUPCAKES

It's fun to prepare individual brownie "cupcakes" with a chocolaty surprise inside. These are the perfect treat to whip up for school parties. My goddaughter asks me to make them every year for her birthday to share with classmates, and they're always a hit!

—Pamela Lute, Mercersburg, Pennsylvania

1/3	cup butter, softened
1	cup sugar
2	eggs
1	teaspoon vanilla extract
3/4	cup all-purpose flour
1/2	cup baking cocoa
1/4	teaspoon baking powder
1/4	teaspoon salt
9	milk chocolate kisses

◆ In a large bowl, cream butter and sugar. Beat in eggs and vanilla; mix well. Combine flour, cocoa, baking powder and salt; add to the creamed mixture and mix well.

◆ Fill paper- or foil-lined muffin cups two-thirds full. Place a chocolate kiss, tip end down, in the center of each. Bake at 350° for 20-25 minutes or until top of brownie springs back when lightly touched.

YIELD: 9 SERVINGS.

Blend Batter Better

Be careful to not overmix your muffin batter as it can cause the muffins to "peak" or form pointy tops. As a general rule, the dry ingredients should be combined first; then stir in the liquid ingredients just until moistened. It's normal for a few lumps to remain in the batter.

MORNING MAPLE MUFFINS

Maple combines with a subtle touch of cinnamon and nuts to give these muffins the flavor of a hearty pancake breakfast. Serve them with maple butter and a hot cup of coffee or tea to start your day off right.

—Elizabeth Talbot, Lexington, Kentucky

2	cups all-purpose flour
1/2	cup packed brown sugar
2	teaspoons baking powder
1/2	teaspoon salt
3/4	cup milk
1/2	cup butter, melted
1/2	cup maple syrup
1/4	cup sour cream
1	egg
1/2	teaspoon vanilla extract

TOPPING:

3	tablespoons all-purpose flour
3	tablespoons sugar
2	tablespoons chopped nuts
1/2	teaspoon ground cinnamon
2	tablespoons cold butter

◆ In a large bowl, combine the flour, brown sugar, baking powder and salt. In another bowl, combine the milk, butter, syrup, sour cream, egg and vanilla. Stir into the dry ingredients just until moistened.

◆ Fill greased or paper-lined muffin cups two-thirds full. For topping, combine the flour, sugar, nuts and cinnamon; cut in butter until crumbly. Sprinkle over batter. Bake at 400° for 16-20 minutes or until muffins are done. Cool for 5 minutes before removing from pans to wire racks.

YIELD: 16 SERVINGS.

ORANGE APPLESAUCE CUPCAKES

Kids of all ages rave about these fruity cupcakes. I've been making them for 25 years to serve at potlucks, church picnics and family suppers. For a tasty variation, substitute crushed pineapple for the applesauce.

—Janis Plourde, Smooth Rock Falls, Ontario

6	tablespoons butter, softened
1	cup packed brown sugar
1	egg
1/2	cup unsweetened applesauce
1	teaspoon vanilla extract
1	teaspoon grated orange peel
1	cup all-purpose flour
1	teaspoon baking powder
1/2	teaspoon salt
1/4	teaspoon baking soda
1/2	cup chopped pecans

FROSTING:

1/4	cup butter, softened
2	cups confectioners' sugar
1-1/2	teaspoons grated orange peel
2	to 4 teaspoons orange juice

◆ In a large bowl, cream the butter and brown sugar until light and fluffy. Beat in egg. Beat in applesauce, vanilla and orange peel. Combine the flour, baking powder, salt and baking soda; gradually add to creamed mixture until blended. Stir in pecans.

◆ Fill paper-lined muffin cups half full. Bake at 350° for 20-25 minutes or until a toothpick comes out clean. Cool cupcakes for 10 minutes before removing from pan to a wire rack to cool completely.

◆ For frosting, in a small bowl, cream butter and sugar until light and fluffy. Add orange peel and enough orange juice to achieve spreading consistency. Frost cupcakes.

YIELD: 12 SERVINGS.

ORANGE BLUEBERRY MUFFINS

With their refreshing blend of citrus and blueberry flavors, these tender muffins are perfect for breakfast or a snack. My mother and husband really enjoy the sweet nut topping on these treats.

—*Janice Baker, London, Kentucky*

1	cup quick-cooking oats
1	cup orange juice
3	cups all-purpose flour
1	cup sugar
2-1/2	teaspoons baking powder
1	teaspoon salt
1/2	teaspoon baking soda
1	cup canola oil
3	eggs, beaten
1-1/2	cups fresh *or* frozen blueberries
1-1/2	teaspoons grated orange peel

TOPPING:

1/2	cup chopped walnuts
1/3	cup sugar
1	teaspoon ground cinnamon

◆ In a small bowl, combine the oats and orange juice. In a large bowl, combine the flour, sugar, baking powder, salt and baking soda. Combine the oil, eggs and oat mixture; stir into dry ingredients just until moistened. Fold in blueberries and orange peel.

◆ Fill paper-lined muffin cups two-thirds full. Combine the topping ingredients; sprinkle over batter. Bake at 400° for 15-20 minutes or until a toothpick comes out clean. Cool for 5 minutes before removing from pans to wire racks.

YIELD: 18 SERVINGS.

Editor's Note: If using frozen blueberries, do not thaw before adding to batter.

FUDGY BANANA MUFFINS

We love the flavor combination of chocolate and banana. Once, when I had no chocolate chips on hand, I made these delicious muffins with chunks of chocolate bars instead. My husband likes them even better this way, since they have big bites of chocolate.

—*Kristin Wagner, Spokane, Washington*

1-1/4	cups all-purpose flour
1	cup whole wheat flour
3/4	cup packed brown sugar
1-1/2	teaspoons baking powder
1	teaspoon baking soda
1/4	teaspoon salt
3	medium ripe bananas, mashed
1-1/4	cups milk
1	egg
1	tablespoon canola oil
2	teaspoons vanilla extract
6	milk chocolate candy bars (1.55 ounces *each*)

◆ In a bowl, combine the flours, brown sugar, baking powder, baking soda and salt. In another bowl, combine bananas, milk, egg, canola oil and vanilla; stir into dry ingredients just until moistened.

◆ Fill greased or paper-lined muffin cups one-third full. Break each candy bar into 12 pieces; place two pieces in each muffin cup. Top with remaining batter. Chop remaining candy bar pieces; sprinkle over batter. Bake at 400° for 15 minutes or until a toothpick inserted in the muffin comes out clean. Cool for 5 minutes before removing from pans to wire racks.

YIELD: 18 SERVINGS.

SWEET RASPBERRY MUFFINS

I like to linger over a cup of coffee and a warm sweet treat on weekend mornings. These moist muffins are perfect because making them ties up so little time in the kitchen. I also serve them with holiday meals for something different.

—*Teresa Raab, Tustin, Michigan*

2	cups biscuit/baking mix
2	tablespoons sugar
1/4	cup cold butter
2/3	cup milk
1/4	cup raspberry jam

GLAZE:

1/2	cup confectioners' sugar
2	teaspoons warm water
1/4	teaspoon vanilla extract

◆ In a bowl, combine biscuit mix and sugar. Cut in cold butter until the mixture resembles coarse crumbs. Stir in milk just until moistened (batter will be thick).

◆ Spoon about 1 tablespoon of batter into 12 paper-lined muffin cups. Top with 1 teaspoon jam. Spoon the remaining batter (about 1 tablespoon each) over jam. Bake at 425° for 12-14 minutes or until lightly browned. Cool in pans for 5 minutes.

◆ Meanwhile, in a small bowl, combine glaze ingredients until smooth. Remove muffins to a wire rack. Drizzle with glaze.

YIELD: 12 SERVINGS.

Delicious by the Dozen

TURN TO THESE delectable goodies the next time you need to create an effortless treat that will please a crowd. From yummy cupcakes and sweet muffins to melt-in-your-mouth mini breads, any one of these big-batch favorites is bound to be a hit at your next picnic, potluck or bake sale.

LEMON CURD CUPCAKES, P. 86

DREAM CUPCAKES

My grandchildren love these blissful, cream-filled cupcakes. They're a special treat, and I can whip them up in a jiffy.

—*Dorothy Bahlmann, Clarksville, Iowa*

1	package (18-1/4 ounces) chocolate cake mix
2	packages (3 ounces *each*) cream cheese, softened
1/3	cup sugar
1	egg
1/8	teaspoon salt
1	cup (6 ounces) semisweet chocolate chips
1/4	cup flaked coconut, optional

◆ Prepare cake mix according to package directions for cupcakes. Fill paper-lined muffin cups half full. In a large bowl, beat cream cheese and sugar until fluffy. Beat in egg and salt until smooth. Stir in chocolate chips and coconut if desired.

◆ Drop about 2 teaspoonfuls of cream cheese mixture into the center of each cupcake. Bake at 350° for 25-30 minutes or until cake springs back when lightly touched. Cool for 5 minutes before removing from pans to wire racks. Store in the refrigerator.

YIELD: 18 SERVINGS.

TRAIL MIX MUFFINS

These hearty muffins blend granola, fruit, nuts and chocolate chips. They're perfect for breakfast-on-the-go or any time you need a lift.

—*Patricia Jones, Hugo, Colorado*

2-1/4	cups all-purpose flour
1	cup granola cereal without raisins
3/4	cup packed brown sugar
2	teaspoons baking powder
1/2	teaspoon salt
2	eggs
1	cup milk
3/4	cup canola oil
1	teaspoon vanilla extract
1/2	cup miniature semisweet chocolate chips
1/2	cup chopped dry roasted peanuts
1/2	cup raisins
1/2	cup chopped dried apricots

◆ In a large bowl, combine the flour, cereal, brown sugar, baking powder and salt. In another bowl, beat the eggs, milk, oil and vanilla; stir into dry ingredients just until moistened. Fold in the chocolate chips, peanuts, raisins and apricots.

◆ Fill greased or paper-lined muffin cups three-fourths full. Bake at 375° for 15-18 minutes or until a toothpick comes out clean. Cool for 5 minutes before removing from pans to wire racks. Serve warm.

YIELD: 18 SERVINGS.

ZUCCHINI CHIP BREAD

You'll love these mild orange-flavored loaves that are chock-full of chocolate chips, nuts and spices. This bread is so easy to stir up, yet it tastes like you spent hours in the kitchen.

—Edie DeSpain, Logan, Utah

3 cups all-purpose flour
2 cups sugar
1 teaspoon baking soda
1 teaspoon salt
1 teaspoon ground nutmeg
1/2 teaspoon ground cinnamon
1/4 teaspoon baking powder
3 eggs
1/2 cup unsweetened applesauce
1/2 cup canola oil
1 tablespoon grated orange peel
2 teaspoons vanilla extract
2 cups shredded zucchini
1 cup chopped walnuts
1 cup (6 ounces) semisweet chocolate chips

◆ In a large bowl, combine the flour, sugar, baking soda, salt, nutmeg, cinnamon and baking powder. In another bowl, beat the eggs, apple-sauce, oil, orange peel and vanilla. Stir into the dry ingredients just until moistened. Fold in the zucchini, nuts and chocolate chips. Transfer to two greased 8-in. x 4-in. x 2-in. loaf pans.

◆ Bake at 350° for 55-60 minutes or until a toothpick inserted near the center comes out clean. Cool for 10 minutes before removing from pans to wire racks to cool completely.

YIELD: 2 LOAVES.

CHOCOLATE CHERRY CUPCAKES

These special treats with a fruity surprise inside are quick to fix with a convenient cake mix. They make a tasty dessert or midnight snack.

—*Bertille Cooper, California, Maryland*

1 package (18-1/4 ounces) chocolate cake mix

1-1/3 cups water

1/2 cup canola oil

3 eggs

1 can (21 ounces) cherry pie filling

1 can (16 ounces) vanilla frosting

◆ In a large bowl, combine the cake mix, water, oil and eggs; beat on low speed for 30 seconds. Beat on medium for 2 minutes.

◆ Spoon batter by 1/4 cupfuls into paper-lined muffin cups. Spoon a rounded teaspoon of pie filling onto the center of each cupcake. Set remaining pie filling aside.

◆ Bake at 350° for 20-25 minutes or until a toothpick inserted on an angle toward the center comes out clean. Remove from pans to wire racks to cool completely.

◆ Frost cupcakes; top with one cherry from pie filling. Serve additional pie filling with cupcakes or refrigerate for another use.

YIELD: 24 SERVINGS.

SWIRLED SPICE LOAVES

Pumpkin pie spice and molasses season these two down-home loaves. The tender marbled slices taste as great as they look. They're a hit at bake sales, too.

—Nancy Zimmerman, Cape May Court House, New Jersey

2	cups all-purpose flour
1-1/3	cups sugar
2	teaspoons baking powder
3/4	teaspoon salt
3	eggs
1-1/4	cups heavy whipping cream
2	tablespoons molasses
3	teaspoons vanilla extract
1-1/2	teaspoons pumpkin pie spice

◆ In a bowl, combine the flour, sugar, baking powder and salt. Beat the eggs and cream; stir into dry ingredients just until combined. Remove 1-1/2 cups batter to another bowl; stir in the molasses, vanilla and pumpkin pie spice until blended.

◆ Spoon a fourth of the molasses batter into each of two greased 8-in. x 4-in. x 2-in. loaf pans. Top each with a fourth of the plain batter. Repeat layers; cut through batter with a knife to swirl.

◆ Bake at 350° for 45-50 minutes or until a toothpick inserted near the center comes out clean. Cool for 10 minutes before removing from pans to wire racks.

YIELD: 2 LOAVES.

GLAZED LEMON MUFFINS

Offer these at any time of year—and watch folks come back for more! The crumb topping and glaze complement the lemony muffins.

—Carol Stevison, Akron, Ohio

1-1/2	cups all-purpose flour
1-1/2	cups sugar
1/4	cup cold butter

MUFFINS:

1-1/2	cups butter, softened
3	cups sugar
6	eggs
1-1/2	cups (12 ounces) sour cream
3	tablespoons lemon juice
2	tablespoons grated lemon peel
4-1/2	cups all-purpose flour
1/2	teaspoon baking soda
1/2	teaspoon salt

GLAZE:

3/4	cup confectioners' sugar
1/3	cup lemon juice

◆ In a bowl, combine flour and sugar. Cut in butter until crumbly; set aside. For muffins, cream butter and sugar in a bowl. Beat in eggs, sour cream, lemon juice and peel. Combine flour, baking soda and salt; stir into creamed mixture just until moistened.

◆ Fill greased or paper-lined muffin cups two-thirds full. Sprinkle with reserved crumb topping. Bake at 350° for 25-30 minutes or until muffins test done. Cool in pans for 5 minutes before removing to wire racks.

◆ Combine glaze ingredients; drizzle over muffins.

YIELD: 24 SERVINGS.

Mammoth Muffins

Out of paper-lined muffin cups? Our home economists have a simple solution. Simply grease aluminum muffin tins on the bottom and halfway up the sides. The ungreased portion will allow the batter to climb up the sides for a higher muffin.

LEMON CURD CUPCAKES

Homemade lemon curd flavors these tender cupcakes that were made for my brother-in-law's 66th birthday. He loves lemon and gave these a big thumb's up.

—*Kerry Barnett-Amundson, Ocean Park, Washington*

3 tablespoons plus 1-1/2 teaspoons sugar
3 tablespoons lemon juice
4-1/2 teaspoons butter
1 egg, lightly beaten
1 teaspoon grated lemon peel

BATTER:

3/4 cup butter, softened
1 cup sugar
2 eggs
1 teaspoon vanilla extract
1 teaspoon grated lemon peel
1-1/2 cups cake flour
1/2 teaspoon baking powder
1/4 teaspoon baking soda
1/4 teaspoon salt
2/3 cup buttermilk

FROSTING:

2 tablespoons butter, softened
1/2 teaspoon vanilla extract
Pinch salt
2 cups confectioners' sugar
2 to 4 tablespoons milk
Pansies *or* other edible flowers, optional

◆ For lemon curd, in a heavy saucepan, cook and stir the sugar, lemon juice and butter until smooth. Stir a small amount of hot mixture into egg; return all to pan. Bring to a gentle boil, stir-ring constantly; cook 2 minutes longer or until thickened. Stir in lemon peel. Cool for 10 minutes. Cover and chill for 1-1/2 hours or until thickened.

◆ In a large bowl, cream butter and sugar until light and fluffy. Add eggs, one at a time, beating well after each. Add vanilla and lemon peel. Combine the flour, baking powder, baking soda and salt; add to creamed mixture alternately with buttermilk.

◆ Fill paper-lined muffin cups three-fourths full. Bake at 350° for 20-25 minutes or until a toothpick comes out clean. Cool 10 minutes; remove cupcakes from pan to a wire rack to cool completely.

◆ Cut a small hole in the corner of a pastry or plastic bag; insert a small round pastry tip. Fill bag with lemon curd. Insert tip 1 in. into center of each cupcake; fill with curd just until tops of cupcakes begin to crack.

◆ In a small bowl, combine frosting ingredients. Frost cupcakes. Store in the refrigerator. Garnish with edible flowers if desired.

YIELD: 12 SERVINGS.

Editor's Note: You can find confectionery roses in the cake decorating aisle at your grocery store.

RHUBARB STREUSEL MUFFINS

What a pleasure it is to set out a basket of these rhubarb muffins based on a coffee cake recipe. I have six children and two grandsons, so the basket doesn't stay full for very long!

—*Sandra Moreside, Regina, Saskatchewan*

1/2	cup butter, softened
1	cup packed brown sugar
1/2	cup sugar
1	egg
2	cups all-purpose flour
1	teaspoon baking powder
1/2	teaspoon baking soda
1/8	teaspoon salt
1	cup (8 ounces) sour cream
3	cups chopped fresh *or* frozen rhubarb, thawed

TOPPING:

1/2	cup chopped pecans
1/4	cup packed brown sugar
1	teaspoon ground cinnamon
1	tablespoon cold butter

◆ In a large bowl, cream butter and sugars. Add egg; beat well. Combine the flour, baking powder, baking soda and salt; add to creamed mixture alternately with sour cream. Fold in rhubarb.

◆ Fill paper-lined or greased muffin cups three-fourths full. For topping, combine the pecans, brown sugar and cinnamon in a small bowl; cut in butter until crumbly. Sprinkle over batter. Bake at 350° for 22-25 minutes or until a toothpick comes out clean. Cool for 5 minutes before removing from pans to wire racks.

YIELD: 18 SERVINGS.

Editor's Note: If using frozen rhubarb, measure rhubarb while still frozen, then thaw completely. Drain in a colander, but do not press liquid out.

PINEAPPLE CHERRY LOAVES

Pineapple adds a fun twist to this holiday quick bread, plus it makes each bite tender and moist. My family prefers this bread to traditional fruitcake.

—*Dolores Peltier, Warren, Michigan*

1-3/4	cups butter, softened
2	cups sugar
8	eggs
1	teaspoon vanilla extract
3-3/4	cups all-purpose flour
1	teaspoon salt
1	teaspoon baking powder
2	cans (8 ounces *each*) pineapple chunks, drained
1	jar (10 ounces) red maraschino cherries, drained and halved
1	jar (10 ounces) green maraschino cherries, drained and halved
2	cups chopped walnuts

◆ In a bowl, cream butter and sugar. Add eggs, one at a time, beating well after each addition. Beat in vanilla.

◆ Combine the flour, salt and baking powder; add to creamed mixture until well blended. Stir in pineapple, cherries and nuts. Pour into three greased and floured 8-in. x 4-in. x 2-in. loaf pans.

◆ Bake at 325° for 1-1/4 hours or until a toothpick comes out clean. Cool for 10 minutes before removing from pans to wire racks.

YIELD: 3 LOAVES.

PECAN PEAR MUFFINS

These muffins are simply delicious! Filled with pears, pecans and down-home goodness, the sweet treats are terrific with a glass of cold milk or a steaming cup of coffee.

—*Laura Ward, Las Vegas, Nevada*

3 cups all-purpose flour

2 cups sugar

2 teaspoons baking soda

1 teaspoon ground cinnamon

1/2 teaspoon salt

2 eggs

1 cup canola oil

1 teaspoon vanilla extract

4 cups chopped peeled ripe pears (about 6 medium)

1 cup chopped pecans

◆ In a large bowl, combine the flour, sugar, baking soda, cinnamon and salt. In another bowl, combine the eggs, oil and vanilla; stir into dry ingredients just until moistened. Fold in the pears and pecans.

◆ Fill paper-lined muffin cups two-thirds full. Bake at 350° for 25-30 minutes or until a toothpick comes out clean. Cool for 5 minutes before removing from pans to wire racks.

YIELD: 24 SERVINGS.

ZUCCHINI CARROT MUFFINS

I use a basic carrot cake mix to stir up these muffins chock-full of zucchini, nuts and raisins. They make great snacks and are wonderful for dessert when spread with cream cheese frosting.

—*Anita Sterrett, Anchorage, Alaska*

1 package (18 ounces) carrot cake mix

1/2 cup applesauce

1/4 cup canola oil

1 egg

1-1/2 cups shredded zucchini

1/2 cup raisins

1/2 cup chopped pecans

◆ In a large bowl, combine the cake mix, applesauce, oil and egg for 30 seconds; beat on low speed for 30 seconds. Beat on medium for 2 minutes. Stir in the zucchini, raisins and pecans.

◆ Fill greased or paper-lined muffin cups three-fourths full. Bake at 350° for 25-30 minutes or until a toothpick comes out clean. Cool for 10 minutes before removing from pan to a wire rack to cool completely.

YIELD: 16 SERVINGS.

MARASCHINO MINI MUFFINS

These chocolate- and cherry-studded mini muffins are easy to prepare and have a sweet flavor everyone adores. They never last long around our house.

—Stephanie Moon-Martin, Silverdale, Washington

1/3	cup butter, softened
2/3	cup sugar
1	egg
1	cup milk
1	tablespoon maraschino cherry juice
1	teaspoon vanilla extract
1/4	teaspoon almond extract
2-1/2	cups all-purpose flour
4	teaspoons baking powder
3/4	teaspoon salt
1/2	cup vanilla *or* white chips
1/3	cup finely chopped maraschino cherries

◆ In a bowl, cream butter and sugar. Add eggs and mix well. Combine the milk, cherry juice and extracts. Combine the flour, baking powder and salt; add to creamed mixture alternately with milk mixture. Fold in the chips and cherries.

◆ Fill greased or paper-lined miniature muffin cups two-thirds full. Bake at 375° for 12-15 minutes or until a toothpick comes out clean. Cool for 5 minutes before removing from pans to wire racks.

YIELD: 48 SERVINGS.

Pan-demonium

Many muffin and cupcake recipes call for an aluminum baking pan, or muffin tin, which vary in cup size. A mini muffin pan has cups with 1-1/2 inches in diameter and holds 1/8 cup batter. A standard size is about 2-1/2 inches in diameter and holds 1/4 cup batter. Jumbo-size is 3-1/8 inches in diameter and holds 1/2 cup batter.

STRAWBERRY NUT BREAD

This delightful quick bread is a strawberry-lover's delight. I like to make easy sandwiches by spreading the homemade strawberry cream cheese between two slices.

—Eunice Morton, Longview, Texas

2	packages (10 ounces *each*) frozen sweetened sliced strawberries, thawed
3	cups all-purpose flour
2	cups sugar
1	teaspoon baking soda
1	teaspoon salt
1	teaspoon ground cinnamon
4	eggs
1-1/4	cups canola oil
1	teaspoon red food coloring, optional
1-1/4	cups chopped pecans
1	package (8 ounces) cream cheese, softened

◆ Drain strawberries, reserving 1/2 cup juice. Set berries and juice aside. In a large bowl, combine flour, sugar, baking soda, salt and cinnamon. Combine eggs, oil, strawberries and food coloring if desired; stir into dry ingredients just until moistened. Stir in pecans.

◆ Pour into two greased 9-in. x 5-in. x 3-in. loaf pans. Bake at 350° for 55-60 minutes or until a toothpick inserted near the center comes out clean. Cool for 10 minutes; remove from pans to a wire rack.

◆ In a small bowl, beat cream cheese and reserved strawberry juice until fluffy; refrigerate. Serve with the bread.

YIELD: 2 LOAVES; 2 CUPS SPREAD.

BLUEBERRY CREAM MUFFINS

I combined two recipes to create these delicious blueberry-filled muffins. The creamy filling makes each bite a little piece of heaven.

—Shari Zimmerman, Orfordville, Wisconsin

4 cups all-purpose flour

1 cup sugar

6 teaspoons baking powder

1 teaspoon salt

2 eggs

2 cups milk

1/2 cup butter, melted

2 cups fresh *or* frozen blueberries

FILLING:

1 package (8 ounces) cream cheese, softened

1 egg

1/3 cup sugar

Dash salt

◆ In a large bowl, combine the flour, sugar, baking powder and salt. In another bowl, beat the eggs, milk and butter; stir mixture into dry ingredients just until moistened. Fold in the blueberries. Spoon about 2 round tablespoonfuls into greased muffin cups.

◆ In a small bowl, beat cream cheese, egg, sugar and salt; place about 1 tablespoon in the center of each muffin cup (do not spread). Top with remaining batter.

◆ Bake at 375° for 18-20 minutes or until a toothpick inserted in muffin comes out clean. Cool for 10 minutes before removing from pans to wire racks to cool completely.

YIELD: 24 SERVINGS.

Editor's Note: If using frozen blueberries, do not thaw before adding to batter.

CHOCOLATE MINI LOAVES

The moist texture of these mini loaves resembles a pound cake. Each bite is rich and succulent, making this perfect for dessert as well as snacking.
—Elizabeth Downey, Evart, Michigan

1/2	cup butter, softened
2/3	cup packed brown sugar
1	cup (6 ounces) semisweet chocolate chips, melted
2	eggs
2	teaspoons vanilla extract
2-1/2	cups all-purpose flour
1	teaspoon baking powder
1	teaspoon baking soda
1-1/2	cups applesauce
1/2	cup miniature semisweet chocolate chips

GLAZE:

1/2	cup semisweet chocolate chips
1	tablespoon butter
5	teaspoons water
1/2	cup confectioners' sugar
1/4	teaspoon vanilla extract

Dash salt

◆ In a large bowl, cream butter and brown sugar. Add the melted chocolate chips, eggs and vanilla; mix well. Combine the flour, baking powder and baking soda; add to creamed mixture alternately with applesauce.

◆ Divide batter among five greased 5-3/4-in. x 3-in. x 2-in. loaf pans, about 1 cup in each. Bake at 350° for 30-40 minutes or until a toothpick inserted near the center comes out clean. Cool for 10 minutes before removing from pans to wire racks to cool completely.

◆ For glaze, combine the chocolate chips, butter and water in a saucepan; cook and stir over low heat until chocolate is melted. Remove from the heat; stir in confectioners' sugar, vanilla and salt until smooth. Drizzle over cooled loaves.

YIELD: 5 MINI LOAVES.

SECRET KISS CUPCAKES

I earned a merit badge by whipping up these cupcakes for a Cub Scouts meeting. You should have seen the grins when the kids bit into the chocolate kisses in the middle. My husband and grandkids say I don't make them often enough.

—Carol Hillebrenner, Fowler, Illinois

3-1/3   cups all-purpose flour
2   cups sugar
1   cup baking cocoa
2   teaspoons baking soda
1   teaspoon salt
2   cups buttermilk
1   cup butter, melted
2   eggs, lightly beaten
2   teaspoons vanilla extract
30   milk chocolate kisses
1   can (16 ounces) fudge frosting

◆ In a large bowl, combine the flour, sugar, cocoa, baking soda and salt.

Combine the buttermilk, butter, eggs and vanilla. Add to the dry ingredients until blended.

◆ Fill paper-lined muffin cups two-thirds full. Press a chocolate kiss into the center of each cupcake until batter completely covers candy.

◆ Bake at 375° for 20-25 minutes or until a toothpick inserted into the cakes comes out clean. Cool for 10 minutes before removing the cupcakes from pans to wire racks to cool completely. Frost cupcakes.

YIELD: 18 SERVINGS.

CHOCOLATE CHIP PUMPKIN BREAD

A touch of cinnamon helps blend the chocolate and pumpkin flavors you'll find in this tender bread. And since the recipe makes two loaves, you can send one to a bake sale and keep one at home for your family to enjoy.

—Lora Stanley, Bennington, Kansas

3   cups all-purpose flour
2   teaspoons ground cinnamon
1   teaspoon salt
1   teaspoon baking soda
4   eggs
2   cups sugar
2   cups canned pumpkin
1-1/2   cups canola oil
1-1/2   cups (6 ounces) semisweet chocolate chips

◆ In a large bowl, combine the flour, cinnamon, salt and baking soda. In another bowl, beat the eggs, sugar, pumpkin and oil. Stir into dry ingredients just until moistened. Fold in chocolate chips.

◆ Pour the batter into two greased 8-in. x 4-in. x 2-in. loaf pans. Bake at 350° for 60-70 minutes or until a toothpick inserted near the center comes out clean. Cool for 10 minutes before removing from pans to wire racks.

YIELD: 2 LOAVES.

ORANGE BANANA NUT BREAD

This variation of traditional banana bread is tasty and simple to fix. The juice gives it a splash of orange flavor making it perfect for breakfast or brunch.

—*Barbara Roethlisberger, Shepherd, Michigan*

1-1/2 cups sugar
3 tablespoons canola oil
2 eggs
3 medium ripe bananas, mashed (about 1-1/4 cups)
3/4 cup orange juice
3 cups all-purpose flour
1-1/2 teaspoons baking powder
1-1/2 teaspoons baking soda
1/2 teaspoon salt
1 cup chopped walnuts

◆ In a bowl, combine the sugar, oil and eggs; mix well. Stir in bananas and orange juice. Combine the dry ingredients; add to banana mixture, beating just until moistened. Stir in walnuts. Pour into two greased 8-in. x 4-in. x 2-in. loaf pans.

◆ Bake at 325° for 50-60 minutes or until a toothpick inserted near the center comes out clean. Cool for 10 minutes; remove from pans to a wire rack to cool completely.

YIELD: 2 LOAVES.

FROSTED PUMPKIN MUFFINS

Jazz up pound cake mix with some canned pumpkin and pumpkin pie spice to create these sweet muffins. They're so good, even picky eaters cannot seem to get enough. Serve them without the frosting or nuts and you'll still get rave reviews.

—*Samantha Callahan, Muncie, Indiana*

1 package (16 ounces) pound cake mix
1 cup canned pumpkin
2 eggs
1/3 cup water
2 teaspoons pumpkin pie spice
1 teaspoon baking soda
1 can (16 ounces) cream cheese frosting
1/2 cup finely chopped pecans, optional

◆ In a large bowl, combine the cake mix, pumpkin, eggs, water, pumpkin pie spice and baking soda; beat on low speed for 30 seconds. Beat on medium for 2 minutes.

◆ Fill greased or paper-lined muffin cups two-thirds full. Bake at 350° for 18-22 minutes or until a toothpick comes out clean. Cool for 5 minutes before removing from pans to wire racks to cool completely.

◆ Frost muffins. Sprinkle with pecans if desired. Store in the refrigerator.

YIELD: 18 SERVINGS.

STRAWBERRY MUFFINS

These luscious oven treats are sweet and flavorful because they're made with lots of strawberries. The cinnamon-honey spread adds the perfect finishing touch.

—Phyllis Carlson, Gardner, Kansas

> 3   cups all-purpose flour
>
> 2   cups sugar
>
> 1   tablespoon ground cinnamon
>
> 1   teaspoon baking soda
>
> 1   teaspoon salt
>
> 2   cups frozen sweetened strawberries, thawed, undrained
>
> 1   cup canola oil
>
> 3   eggs, beaten
>
> 1/4   to 1/2 teaspoon red food coloring, optional
>
> 1-1/2   cups chopped pecans, optional

CINNAMON-HONEY SPREAD:

> 1/2   cup butter, softened
>
> 1   cup confectioners' sugar
>
> 1/4   cup honey
>
> 1/4   teaspoon ground cinnamon

◆ In a large bowl, combine flour, sugar, cinnamon, baking soda and salt. In another bowl, mix strawberries, oil, eggs and food coloring if desired; stir into dry ingredients just until moistened. Fold in pecans if desired.

◆ Fill greased muffin cups three-fourths full. Bake at 375° for 15-18 minutes or until muffins test done.

◆ Meanwhile, combine spread ingredients in a small bowl; beat until blended. Serve with the muffins. Store spread in the refrigerator.

YIELD: 18 SERVINGS; 3/4 CUP SPREAD.

BUTTERSCOTCH MUFFINS

Butterscotch pudding gives a distinctive flavor to these muffins topped with sweet brown sugar and crunchy nuts. My son loves them so much he decided to enter the recipe in his 4-H competition and won first prize.

—Jill Hazelton, Hamlet, Indiana

2 cups all-purpose flour

1 cup sugar

1 package (3.4 ounces) instant butterscotch pudding mix

1 package (3.4 ounces) instant vanilla pudding mix

2 teaspoons baking powder

1 teaspoon salt

1 cup water

4 eggs

3/4 cup canola oil

1 teaspoon vanilla extract

TOPPING:

2/3 cup packed brown sugar

1/2 cup chopped pecans

2 teaspoons ground cinnamon

◆ In a large bowl, combine the flour, sugar, pudding mixes, baking powder and salt. Combine the water, eggs, oil and vanilla; stir into the dry ingredients just until moistened.

◆ Fill greased or paper-lined muffin cups two-thirds full. Combine the topping ingredients; sprinkle over batter. Bake at 350° for 15-20 minutes or until a toothpick comes out clean. Cool for 5 minutes before removing from pans to wire racks.

YIELD: 18 SERVINGS.

COCONUT ORANGE CUPCAKES

This tried-and-true recipe features the delicate tastes of orange, white chocolate and coconut in an easy dessert worthy of company. It yields 2 dozen delicious cupcakes with a pretty topping.

—*Donna Justin, Sparta, Wisconsin*

1	cup sugar
2/3	cup canola oil
2	eggs
1	cup orange juice
3	cups all-purpose flour
1	tablespoon baking powder
1	teaspoon baking soda
3/4	teaspoon salt
1	can (11 ounces) mandarin oranges, drained
1	cup vanilla *or* white chips

TOPPING:

1	cup flaked coconut
1/3	cup sugar
2	tablespoons butter, melted

◆ In a large bowl, beat the sugar, oil, eggs and orange juice until well blended. Combine the flour, baking powder, baking soda and salt; gradually stir into orange juice mixture just until moistened. Fold in oranges and chips.

◆ Fill paper-lined muffin cups two-thirds full. In a small bowl, combine topping ingredients; sprinkle over cupcakes. Bake at 375° for 15-20 minutes or until golden brown. Remove to wire racks to cool.

YIELD: 24 SERVINGS.

FRESH PEAR BREAD

When our tree branches are loaded with ripe juicy pears, I treat my family and friends to loaves of this cinnamony bread richly studded with walnuts. I always receive rave reviews and multiple requests for the recipe.

—*Linda Patrick, Houston, Texas*

3	eggs
1-1/2	cups sugar
3/4	cup canola oil
1	teaspoon vanilla extract
3	cups all-purpose flour
2	teaspoons baking powder
2	teaspoons ground cinnamon
1	teaspoon baking soda
1	teaspoon salt
4	cups finely chopped peeled ripe pears (about 4 medium)
1	teaspoon lemon juice
1	cup chopped walnuts

◆ In a bowl, combine the eggs, sugar, oil and vanilla; mix well. Combine flour, baking powder, cinnamon, baking soda and salt; stir into the egg mixture just until moistened. Toss pears with lemon juice. Stir pears and walnuts into batter (batter will be thick).

◆ Spoon into two greased 9-in. x 5-in. x 3-in. loaf pans. Bake at 350° for 55-60 minutes or until a toothpick inserted near the center comes out clean. Cool for 10 minutes before removing from pans to wire racks.

YIELD: 2 LOAVES.

Mini Breads

IN ADDITION to the scrumptious cupcake and muffin recipes featured in this book, we've included this bonus chapter of delicious mini breads. Heartwarming, irresistible and ready in a jiffy, slices of these breads make wonderful additions to any goodie platter.

BERRY MINI BREADS, P. 104

BANANA SPLIT BREAD

Good old banana bread is delightfully dressed up in this version, studded with chocolate chips and crunchy pecans. I serve yummy slices at the holiday brunch I plan annually for my relatives.

—*Shelly Rynearson, Dousman, Wisconsin*

1/2	cup butter, softened
1	cup sugar
1	egg
1	cup mashed ripe bananas (about 2 large)
3	tablespoons milk
2	cups all-purpose flour
1	teaspoon baking powder
1/2	teaspoon baking soda
1	cup (6 ounces) semisweet chocolate chips
1/2	cup chopped pecans

In a large bowl, cream butter and sugar until light and fluffy. Beat in egg. In a small bowl, combine bananas and milk. Combine the flour, baking powder and baking soda; add to creamed mixture alternately with banana mixture. Fold in chips and pecans.

Pour into a greased 9-in. x 5-in. x 3-in. loaf pan. Bake at 350° for 60-70 minutes or until a toothpick inserted near the center comes out clean. Cool for 10 minutes before removing from pan to a wire rack to cool completely.

YIELD: 1 LOAF.

COCONUT LOAF

I suggest a cup of tea when enjoying a slice of this cake-like bread. It does well at bake sales and is a wonderful hostess gift—particularly for coconut lovers.

—*Mary Ann Dudek, Cleveland, Ohio*

1/2	cup butter, softened
1	cup sugar
2	eggs
1	teaspoon vanilla extract
2	cups all-purpose flour
2	teaspoons baking powder
1/2	teaspoon salt
3/4	cup milk
1-1/4	cups flaked coconut

In a bowl, cream butter and sugar. Add eggs, one at a time, beating well after each addition. Beat in vanilla. Combine the flour, baking powder and salt; add to creamed mixture alternately with milk. Stir in coconut.

Pour into a greased 9-in. x 5-in. x 3-in. loaf pan. Bake at 350° for 1 hour or until a toothpick inserted near the center comes out clean. Cool for 10 minutes before removing from pan to a wire rack to cool completely.

YIELD: 1 LOAF.

APRICOT MINI LOAVES

These lightly spiced loaves are full of apricot-walnut flavor with a honey and clove glaze. My daughter helped me whip up the tiny loaves with ingredients we had on hand, and they were simply delectable.

—Kelly Koutahi, Moore, Oklahoma

1	egg, lightly beaten
6	tablespoons milk
5	tablespoons butter, melted
4-1/2	teaspoons honey
1/2	teaspoon vanilla extract
1	cup pancake mix
1/4	cup finely chopped walnuts
1/4	cup finely chopped dried apricots
2	tablespoons raisins

GLAZE:

1/2	cup confectioners' sugar
1	teaspoon honey
1/8	teaspoon ground cloves
2	to 3 teaspoons milk

In a bowl, combine the egg, milk, butter, honey and vanilla extract; stir in the pancake mix just until moistened. Fold in the walnuts, apricots and raisins.

Pour into two greased 4-1/2-in. x 2-1/2-in. x 1-1/2-in. loaf pans. Bake at 350° for 22-28 minutes or until a toothpick inserted near the center comes out clean. Cool for 5 minutes before removing from pans to wire racks. In a small bowl, combine the glaze ingredients. Drizzle over warm loaves. Cool.

YIELD: 2 LOAVES.

RASPBERRY LEMON LOAF

This easy-to-prepare quick bread is flavored with tangy lemon peel and fresh raspberries. The loaf is refreshing as a snack, at breakfast...or any time of day.

—Carol Dodds, Aurora, Ontario

1-3/4   cups all-purpose flour
1/2   cup sugar
1   teaspoon baking powder
1/2   teaspoon baking soda
1/2   teaspoon salt
1   egg
2   egg whites
1   cup reduced-fat lemon yogurt
1/4   cup canola oil
2   teaspoons grated lemon peel
1   cup fresh raspberries

In a large bowl, combine the dry ingredients. In another bowl, whisk together the egg, egg whites, yogurt, oil and lemon peel. Add to the dry ingredients just until moistened. Fold in the raspberries.

Transfer to an 8-in. x 4-in. x 2-in. loaf pan coated with cooking spray. Bake at 350° for 60-65 minutes or until a toothpick inserted near the center comes out clean. Cool for 10 minutes before removing from pan to a wire rack to cool completely.

YIELD: 1 LOAF.

BUTTERMILK CHOCOLATE BREAD

This rich cake-like bread and its creamy chocolate honey butter make a great brunch item and also goes well on a dinner buffet. I entered this cherished recipe in a local cooking contest and won a "Best in Category" award.

—*Patrice Bruwer, Grand Rapids, Michigan*

1/2   cup butter, softened
1   cup sugar
2   eggs
1-1/2   cups all-purpose flour
1/2   cup baking cocoa
1/2   teaspoon salt
1/2   teaspoon baking powder
1/2   teaspoon baking soda
1   cup buttermilk
1/3   cup chopped pecans

CHOCOLATE HONEY BUTTER:

1/2   cup butter, softened
2   tablespoons honey
2   tablespoons chocolate syrup

In a bowl, cream butter and sugar. Add eggs, one at a time, beating well after each addition. Combine the flour, cocoa, salt, baking powder and baking soda; add to creamed mixture alternately with buttermilk. Fold in pecans.

Pour mixture into a greased 9-in. x 5-in. x 3-in. loaf pans. Bake at 350° for 55-60 minutes or until a toothpick inserted near the center comes out clean. Cool for 10 minutes before removing from pan to a wire rack.

In a small bowl, beat butter until fluffy. Add honey and chocolate syrup; mix well. Serve with the bread.

YIELD: 1 LOAF; 1/2 CUP BUTTER.

GUMDROP BREAD

Colorful gumdrops make these fun miniature loaves perfect for holiday gift-giving. I always bake this moist bread at Christmas and Easter, but I also get requests from friends and family throughout the year.

—*Linda Samaan, Fort Wayne, Indiana*

3   cups biscuit/baking mix
2/3   cup sugar
1   egg
1-1/4   cups milk
1-1/2   cups chopped nuts
1   cup chopped gumdrops

In a bowl, combine biscuit mix and sugar. In another bowl, beat the egg and milk; add to dry ingredients and stir well. Add nuts and gumdrops; stir just until mixed. Pour mixture into three greased 5-3/4-in. x 3-in. x 2-in. loaf pans.

Bake at 350° for 35 minutes or until a toothpick inserted near the center comes out clean. Cool for 10 minutes; remove loaves from pans to wire racks to cool completely.

YIELD: 3 MINI LOAVES.

Make-Ahead Bread

It's easy to surprise your family with a slice of home-baked bread at a moment's notice! Just bake a loaf when you have the time, then freeze it for future use. Most breads are fine to freeze for up to one or two months. Serve bread at room temperature or if you prefer it warm, simply wrap the bread in foil and bake at 350° for 15 to 20 minutes.

BERRY MINI BREADS

A package containing this buttery, sweet-tart bread and its recipe was dropped at our doorstep one evening during the holidays. It was so tasty and festive that it has become a tradition at our house. Now we also leave the same gift on many doorsteps not only at Christmas, but throughout the year.

—Heidi Naylor, Boise, Idaho

1/2 cup butter, softened
1 cup sugar
2 eggs
3 cups all-purpose flour
1 teaspoon baking soda
1 teaspoon baking powder
1 teaspoon salt
1 cup buttermilk
1 cup whole-berry cranberry sauce
1 cup fresh *or* frozen blueberries

In a bowl, cream butter and sugar. Add the eggs, one at a time, beating well after each addition. Combine dry ingredients; add to the creamed mixture alternately with buttermilk. Stir in cranberry sauce and blueberries. Pour into four greased 5-3/4-in. x 3-in. x 2-in. loaf pans.

Bake at 350° for 25-30 minutes or until a toothpick inserted near the center comes out clean. Cool for 10 minutes before removing from pans to wire racks.

YIELD: 4 LOAVES.

RAISIN BANANA BREAD

My aunt shared the recipe for this tasty bread with me. Grated carrots and zucchini, plus raisins and walnuts, bring a wonderful blend of flavors to this out-of-the-ordinary banana bread.

—Margaret Hinman, Burlington, Iowa

3 cups all-purpose flour
2 cups sugar
1 teaspoon baking powder
1 teaspoon salt
1 teaspoon pumpkin pie spice
1/2 teaspoon baking soda
1/2 teaspoon ground cinnamon
3 eggs
1 cup canola oil
2 teaspoons vanilla extract
1 cup grated zucchini
1 cup grated carrot
1/2 cup mashed ripe banana
1/2 cup raisins
1/2 cup chopped walnuts

In a bowl, combine the first seven ingredients. Add eggs, oil and vanilla; mix well. Stir in zucchini, carrot, banana, raisins and nuts.

Pour into four greased and floured 5-in. x 3-in. x 2-in. loaf pans. Bake at 350° for 45-48 minutes or until a toothpick inserted near the center comes out clean. Cool for 10 minutes; remove from pans to wire racks.

YIELD: 4 LOAVES.

SWEET TROPICAL LOAVES

These pineapple-coconut loaves are so moist that sometimes I don't even bother to glaze them. The golden bread gets its tender, cake-like texture from a handy boxed cake mix.

—Sybil Brown, Highland, California

1　**package (18-1/4 ounces) yellow cake mix**

1　**can (8 ounces) crushed pineapple, undrained**

1　**cup evaporated milk**

2　**eggs**

1/2　**teaspoon ground nutmeg**

1/2　**cup flaked coconut**

GLAZE:

1-1/2　**cups confectioners' sugar**

2　**tablespoons milk**

1　**to 2 drops coconut extract, optional**

2　**tablespoons flaked coconut, toasted**

In a large bowl, combine the first five ingredients; beat on low speed just for 30 seconds. Beat on high for 2 minutes. Stir in coconut.

Pour into two greased 8-in. x 4-in. x 2-in. loaf pans. Bake at 325° for 45-50 minutes or until a toothpick inserted near the center comes out clean. Cool for 10 minutes before removing from pans to wire racks to cool completely.

For glaze, in a small bowl, combine sugar and milk until smooth. Add extract if desired. Drizzle over loaves; sprinkle with coconut.

YIELD: 2 LOAVES.

GOLDEN OATMEAL BREAD

This recipe, developed by our home economists, is great for breakfast or dessert. Slice into this old-fashioned loaf and savor the subtle oat flavor, crunchy pecans and sweet raisins, with just a hint of cinnamon.

—Taste of Home Test Kitchen

1	cup all-purpose flour
3/4	cup plus 1 tablespoon quick-cooking oats, *divided*
1/2	cup whole wheat flour
1/2	cup sugar
2	teaspoons baking powder
3/4	teaspoon baking soda
1/2	teaspoon ground cinnamon
3/4	cup unsweetened applesauce
1	egg
1-1/2	teaspoons vanilla extract
1/3	cup golden raisins
1/3	cup chopped pecans, toasted

In a large bowl, combine all-purpose flour, 3/4 cup of oats, whole wheat flour, sugar, baking powder, baking soda and cinnamon. In another bowl, combine the applesauce, egg and vanilla; stir into dry ingredients just until moistened. Fold in raisins and pecans.

Pour into an 8-in. x 4-in. x 2-in. loaf pan coated with cooking spray. Sprinkle with remaining oats. Bake at 325° for 50-55 minutes or until a toothpick inserted near the center comes out clean. Cool for 10 minutes before removing bread from pan to wire rack.

YIELD: 1 LOAF.

APPLE CRANBERRY BREAD

Cranberries lend a burst of tartness and bright color to this moist quick bread. Dotted with crunchy nuts, slices are good for breakfast with a cup of coffee or as a snack any time of day.

—*Phyllis Schmalz, Kansas City, Kansas*

- 2   eggs
- 3/4   cup sugar
- 2   tablespoons canola oil
- 1-1/2   cups all-purpose flour
- 1-1/2   teaspoons baking powder
- 1   teaspoon ground cinnamon
- 1/2   teaspoon baking soda
- 1/2   teaspoon salt
- 2   cups chopped peeled tart apples
- 1   cup fresh *or* frozen cranberries
- 1/2   cup chopped walnuts

In a bowl, beat the eggs, sugar and oil. Combine the flour, baking powder, cinnamon, baking soda and salt; add to egg mixture just until combined (batter will be very thick). Stir in the apples, cranberries and walnuts.

Transfer to an 8-in. x 4-in. x 2-in. loaf pan coated with cooking spray. Bake at 350° for 60-65 minutes or until a toothpick inserted near the center comes out clean. Cool for 10 minutes before removing from pan to a wire rack to cool completely.

YIELD: 1 LOAF.

LEMON YOGURT LOAF

This delicate tea bread is perfect for a light summer dessert or Sunday brunch. The combination of tart lemon, tangy apricots and sweet icing is simply wonderful.

—*Angela Biggin, Lyons, Illinois*

- 3/4   cup plus 2 teaspoons lemon yogurt, *divided*
- 1/2   cup dried apricots
- 1/2   cup butter, softened
- 3/4   cup plus 2 tablespoons confectioners' sugar, *divided*
- 3   eggs
- 1   tablespoon grated lemon peel
- 2   cups self-rising flour

In a blender, combine 3/4 cup yogurt and apricots; cover and process until smooth. In a bowl, cream the butter and 3/4 cup confectioners' sugar. Beat in the eggs, lemon peel and yogurt mixture; mix well. Add flour just until combined. Spoon into a greased 8-in. x 4-in. x 2-in. loaf pan.

Bake at 325° for 60-65 minutes or until a toothpick inserted near the center comes out clean. Cool for 10 minutes before removing from pan to a wire rack to cool completely. Combine the remaining yogurt and confectioners' sugar; drizzle over loaf.

YIELD: 1 LOAF.

Editor's Note: As a substitute for each cup of self-rising flour, place 1-1/2 teaspoons baking powder and 1/2 teaspoon salt in a measuring cup. Add all-purpose flour to measure 1 cup.

General Recipe Index

*This index lists every recipe by food category and/or major ingredient,
so you can easily locate recipes to suit your needs.*

Alphabetical Index

This index lists every recipe in alphabetical order so you can easily find your favorite recipes.

The elves played with the eggs.

"Be careful, elves," said Little e.

Now the box was heavy.

So Little  found an elephant.

"Hop on," said the elephant.

The elephant went up and down . . .

the eggs fell out of the box.

The elves fell, too.

So did Little .

"That was a bad bump," he said.

"What a mess," said Little .
"Now who will help me
fill my box?"

An Eskimo  came by.

"I will help you
fill your box,"
said the Eskimo.

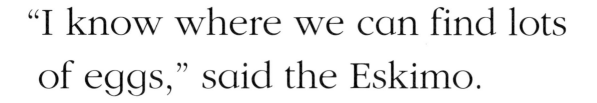

"I know where we can find lots
of eggs," said the Eskimo.

Guess who had eggs,
eggs for Little  ?

Guess who had pretty eggs
for everyone?

elephant

elves

Eskimo

Can you read these words

with Little 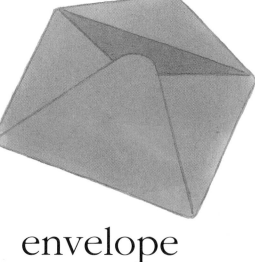 ?

elevator

envelope

Little  has another sound in some words. He says his name, "e."

Can you read these words?
Listen for Little e's name.

eagle

eel

emu

Easter

ABOUT THE AUTHOR AND ILLUSTRATOR

Jane Belk Moncure began her writing career when she was in kindergarten. She has never stopped writing. Many of her children's stories and poems have been published, to the delight of young readers, including her son Jim, whose childhood experiences found their way into many of her books.

Mrs. Moncure's writing is based upon an active career in early childhood education. A recipient of an M.A. degree from Columbia University, Mrs. Moncure has taught and directed nursery, kindergarten, and primary grade programs in California, New York, Virginia, and North Carolina. As a former member of the faculties of Virginia Commonwealth University and the University of Richmond, she taught prospective teachers in early childhood education.

Mrs. Moncure has travelled extensively abroad, studying early childhood programs in the United Kingdom, The Netherlands, and Switzerland. She was the first president of the Virginia Association for Early Childhood Education and received its award for outstanding service to young children.

A resident of North Carolina, Mrs. Moncure is currently a full-time writer and educational consultant. She is married to Dr. James A. Moncure, former vice president of Elon College.

Colin King studied at the Royal College of Art, London. He started his freelance career as an illustrator, working for magazines and advertising agencies.

He began drawing pictures for children's books in 1976 and has illustrated over sixty titles to date.

Included in a wide variety of subjects are a best-selling children's encyclopedia and books about spies and detectives.

His books have been translated into several languages, including Japanese and Hebrew. He has four grown-up children and lives in Suffolk, England, with his wife, three dogs, and a cat.